Rethinking the Femme Fatale in Film Noir

Also by Julie Grossman

A DUE VOCI: THE PHOTOGRAPHY OF RITA HAMMOND
(edited with Ann M. Ryan and Kim Waale, 2003)

Rethinking the Femme Fatale in Film Noir

Ready for Her Close-Up

Julie Grossman

First published 2009 by
PALGRAVE MACMILLAN

Palgrave Macmillan in the UK is an imprint of Macmillan Publishers Limited, registered in England, company number 785998, of Houndmills, Basingstoke, Hampshire RG21 6XS.

Palgrave Macmillan in the US is a division of St Martin's Press LLC, 175 Fifth Avenue, New York, NY 10010.

Palgrave Macmillan is the global academic imprint of the above companies and has companies and representatives throughout the world.

Palgrave® and Macmillan® are registered trademarks in the United States, the United Kingdom, Europe and other countries

ISBN-13: 978-0-230-23328-7   hardback

This book is printed on paper suitable for recycling and made from fully managed and sustained forest sources. Logging, pulping and manufacturing processes are expected to conform to the environmental regulations of the country of origin.

A catalogue record for this book is available from the British Library.

A catalog record for this book is available from the Library of Congress.

10   9   8   7   6   5   4   3   2   1
18   17   16   15   14   13   12   11   10   09

Printed and bound in Great Britain by
CPI Antony Rowe, Chippenham and Eastbourne

As that famous philosopher Dr. Seuss said, "When you are in Love you can't fall asleep because reality is better than your dreams." In that spirit, I dedicate this book to sleeplessness and to Phil and Sophie.

Contents

List of Figures

Acknowledgments

I'd like to thank Jim Hurley, who gave me a starter kit of film noir movies in graduate school at the University of Virginia.

I'd also like to thank my interesting and engaged film noir students at Le Moyne College, who have taught me a lot over the years, especially Jon Bidwell, Aaron Brockler, Laura Chomyn, Danielle Clement, Erin Curley, Michael Donnelly, Kristin Egan, Dave Fisselbrand, Todd Fox, Kori Gerbig, Becky Godridge, Tara Harney, Annabeth Hayes, Juli Hebert, Debbie Hutchison, Kara Keenan, Liza LaLomia, Jill LeClair, Melissa Lee, Ron Martin, Jenn Mentry, Jill Merrell-Mahoney, Adelle Moore, Kelly Morgan, Sarah Morisano, Katie Murak, Khalil Nasiri, Nell O'Hara, Jennifer Orne, Karyn Peroyea, Nicole Roussos, Shreyas Roy, Kate Shannon, Terrence Swiger, Sarah Vitale, and Rain Zebrowski.

Le Moyne's Research and Development Committee supported this project, as did Le Moyne's exceptional provost, Linda LeMura. I am fortunate to have such wonderful colleagues in the English department, and my thanks, also, to the Communication program and to Mike Streissguth. I'm grateful to my friends and colleagues in the dean's office, Jeanne Darby and Carly Colbert, for their support and for putting up with me in the last days of preparing this manuscript.

Many thanks to the UCLA film archive, where I began doing research on film noir some time back, before many of the films I discuss in this project were available on DVD or VHS.

Thanks to Christabel Scaife, my editor at Palgrave Macmillan, for her advice, support, and patience.

Special thanks to Tyler Ochoa for his sage advice and material help.

Thanks to Dave McCall at the British Film Institute and to the wonderful staff at the BFI Library.

Nancy Kauffman at The George Eastman House also helped me immensely in securing images for this book.

A version of Chapter 1 appeared in the *Quarterly Review of Film and Video* 24: 1 (January, 2007). 19–30.

My thanks to the panel chairs and conference organizers, who supported earlier versions and parts of this project, including the International Association of Philosophy and Literature, Katherine Milligan, Mark Osteen, and the Upstate New York Victorian Studies Reading Group. Two conferences in particular helped me enormously in advancing this project: the wonderful 2007 conference called "Cinematicity," hosted at Essex University by Jeff Geiger and Karen Littau and the memorable 2005 conference "Cherchez La Femme: The Cinematic Femme Fatale, Her History and Transmissions," hosted at Exeter University by Helen Hanson and Catherine O'Rawe. This conference, now affectionately referred to as "Google la Femme," was a groundbreaking and richly provocative series of presentations, exchanges, and conversations, as well as the beginning of new friendships.

Finally, I'd especially like to recognize my friends, colleagues, and sister Amy Breiger, for their input and extremely helpful observations in connection with this project at various points in its evolution: Eyal Amiran, Jill Beifuss, Tom Brockelman, Helen Hanson, Chris Warner, Orlando Ocampo, M. J. Devaney, John Paul Riquelme, Michael Davis, Lib Hayes, and especially Ann Ryan, Patrick Keane, Julie Olin-Ammentorp, and Kate Costello-Sullivan.

This project is in memory of Liz Salvagno, whose strength and intellectual passion surely enhanced in some way my desire to write a book about powerful and smart women.

To my great-grandmother "Mommie Sophie," the first female driver in New Haven, Connecticut; to my grandmother Tiny, one of the earliest female lawyers in New York City; to my mother Paula, also a lawyer, a writer, and my first model of a strong woman; to my sister Amy, my first and wisest best friend; to my daughter Sophie, who inherits the gifts of these women and adds to them her own kindness, warmth, energy, wit, and intelligence.

To Phillip Novak, who has helped me profoundly in relation to this project, in all of its many stages. His talent, insight, and companionship are an integral part of this book, and I'm deeply and forever grateful to have him in my life.

Introduction
"No One Mourns the Wicked"

In Alfred Hitchcock's *Notorious* (1946), Devlin (Cary Grant) casts Alicia Huberman (Ingrid Bergman) as a "femme fatale," unable to imagine "that a woman like [her] could ever change her spots." Formerly promiscuous, and sullied by reputation, as well, because of her fascist, recently deceased father, Alicia bears the burden of Dev's judgment and mistrust throughout their sadomasochistic courtship. While the ambiguity of Dev's and Alicia's roles has been recognized by critics such as Donald Spoto (who felicitously refers to Dev as "Prince Not-So-Charming" and Alicia as "Snow Beige" [155]), Alicia's victimization by Devlin, her exploitation by the government men who use her as a pawn to seduce the strangely vulnerable fascist Alex Sebastian (Claude Rains), and her weary resignation to becoming the "fatal" woman, don't tend to register in critical discussions of the film as part of a larger pattern of misreading women in film noir.

Indeed, despite the iconic image of Norma Desmond from *Sunset Boulevard* (1950) claiming that she is "ready for her close-up," from which this study's subtitle is drawn, critics have yet to examine the alleged "femme fatale" in all her complexity. This study undertakes to wear away at the category of the "femme fatale" figure in order to elicit a more nuanced and sympathetic reading of the women too easily branded as "femmes fatales," not only in film criticism but also in popular cultural commentary on sexualized and/or highly intelligent and competent women.

As much film criticism has rehearsed, film noir has been understood in a feminist context in two central ways: first, as a body of texts that give rise to feminist critique; and second, as a celebration of unchecked female power. Laura Mulvey's analysis of the male gaze, first published in *Screen* in 1975, was central to feminist discussions of film noir's

1

potential misogyny. Such insights contributed to larger conversations about cinematic structure, gender representation, and film noir, circling around issues of identity, identification, fantasy, and objectification, and focusing on the extent to which film noir is a "male sphere" and the "femme fatale" figure a projection of male desire and anxiety, an expression of misogyny best expressed by Janey Place in her essay in the first volume of E. Ann Kaplan's *Women in Film Noir* (1978): "Men need to control women's sexuality in order not to be destroyed by it" (reprinted in 2nd edn, Kaplan, 1998, 49). The view that film noir addresses or critiques patriarchy is shared by other feminist film critics, and evolves out of feminist claims in the 1970s (and since) that the "femme fatale" is a projection of postwar male anxiety about changing or ambiguous gender roles.

The extent to which women in noir figure as projections of male desire and anxiety is familiar to us, in large part as a result of the excellent psychoanalytic work on film noir done by feminist film critics and theorists, such as the essays represented in E. Ann Kaplan's indispensable *Women in Film Noir* (1978; 1998), some of the essays in *The Book of Film Noir* (1994), edited by Ian Cameron, Frank Krutnik's *In a Lonely Street* (1991), Mary Ann Doane's *Femmes Fatales* (1991), and the essays collected in Joan Copjec's *Shades of Noir* (1993). However, I want to suggest the limits of psychoanalytic readings which seek to abstract representations of men and women from the social world. While the analysis of Oedipal projection has enriched our understanding of film noir immensely, it has also, over time, resulted in a fixation on the "femme fatale" figure and has stalled fuller understanding of the ways in which class and gender function as crucial factors in representations of women in noir.

My project seeks to turn critical attention away from spectator and gaze theory and the idea of the "femme fatale" and toward examination of narrative, social psychology, and the mise-en-scene in film noir movies that, I argue in this study, reveal that a large majority of the so-called bad women in noir are not demonized in the films in which they appear and are very often shown to be victims: first, of the social rules that dictate gender roles and, second, of reading practices that overidentify with and overinvest in the idea of the "femme fatale."

The continued debate concerning whose fantasy, male or female, is engaged by film noir (central to Copjec's *Shades of Noir* and discussed at some length in the Introduction to the new edition of Kaplan's *Women in Film Noir*) generalizes narrative and images in relation to types, such as the "femme fatale" and the "hard-boiled" male protagonist. Even to argue, as Kaplan does, that "film noir offers a space for the playing out of *various* gender fantasies" (1998,10), developing Elizabeth Cowie's emphasis on the multiplicity of identifications possible in viewing film noir, can elide female stories and the social contexts presented in these films that are so central in generating their meaning and that often determine the fatalistic or traumatic tone of the films. Invoking the framework of fantasy broadens the purview of film noir to an extent that close analysis of the films and their expression and critique of social psychology are neglected, and the conventional values associated with roles such as the "femme fatale" and "hard-boiled" male protagonist are reaffirmed.

Clearly the "femme fatale" is a product of cultural ideation, but this for me is a starting point of analysis, rather than a concluding psychoanalytic insight that leaves the category of the "femme fatale" intact. Fantasies of women are sociohistorically based and thus affected by the position of women in any given historical moment. As Claire Johnston has rightly said, "the myths governing the cinema are no different from those governing other cultural products: they relate to a standard value system informing all cultural systems in a given society" (408). The ambitions and desires of women represented in film noir may express universal psychological factors, but they're surely deeply social, as well. Most "femmes fatales" are sexual, but that's not their main appeal—if it were, *Sunset Boulevard*'s Norma Desmond wouldn't be the central figure in film noir that she is. It is the leading female's commitment to fulfilling her own desires, whatever they may be (sexual, capitalist, maternal), at any cost, that makes her the cynosure, the compelling point of interest for men and women. Film noir movies work to identify their tough women as victims whose strength, perverse by conventional standards, keeps them from submitting to the gendered social institutions that oppress them. It is the dialog between their perversity and their power and these films' illumination of modern women, *femmes modernes* (a phrase I return to repeatedly in this study), that fascinates film viewers.

My concern is that gaze theory has overemphasized women as objects and has mystified their role as social agents because of its reliance on unchanging and unchangeable models of spectatorship, whose schematic approach to the structure of the film fails to take the context and the content of individual films sufficiently into account. While psychological and psychoanalytic readings of film noir do make sense of context in many cases (for example, I contrast two applications of psychological views of borderline personality in Chapter 3), broader attention paid to the social formation of gender represented in these films provides, I think, a crucial context for finding meaning in film noir. When I make reference to projection and fantasy throughout this study, I mean to ground my claims in gender psychology and social distributions of power rather than psychoanalytic structures embedded in cinematic form.

The second feminist view of film noir that has dominated film criticism celebrates the "femme fatale's" unbridled female sexuality and/or female independence. The films, Elizabeth Cowie has said, "afforded women roles which are active, adventurous and driven by sexual desire" (Copjec, 135). The dangerous women in film noir are lawless agents of female desire, rebelling against the patriarchal relegation of women to the domestic sphere where they are deemed passive and valued only in relation to their maternal and wifely vocation.

In Kaplan's first volume of *Women in Film Noir* (1978), alternatives to standard readings of the "femme fatale" as misogynist were explored, such as the thesis that the "femme fatale" is not just misogynist projection but an instance for women of female independence that is powerful because it is "mysterious and unknowable" (Gledhill, 1978, 122). The "femmes fatales" threatens to transgress patriarchy. In this view it is the lack of context provided for the actions of the most recognizable "femmes fatales" (and there are few, I maintain), such as Kathy Moffett, Brigid O'Shaughnessy, or Phyllis Dietrichson that constitutes their transgressive power (a good thing), as opposed to the domestication of the "femme fatale" in *Klute* (1971), Gledhill's target, in which Bree Daniels is disempowered by being subjected to clinical investigation.[1] Bree's power is, Gledhill argues, psychologized away, suggesting an anti-feminist model in "normal" domesticated woman. I think that the film's ending is more ambiguous than this reading suggests; however, Gledhill's interest in the value of the opaque "femme fatale" remains compelling, as an alternative way of understanding the positive value of the "femme fatale's" role as rebel (e.g., I wouldn't want Bridget Gregory from *The Last Seduction* [1994] in my life, but as a representation of unvanquishable, unrapable woman, and in some cases, a symbol of vengeance against male control,[2] she offers a symbol of freedom and power that may be culturally constructive).

On the one hand, I situate myself in connection with the latter group of critics, who see film noir as subversive in its representation of gender. I align myself with Jans Wager, Elizabeth Cowie, and Helen Hanson, who question the notion that noir is primarily a "male preserve" (Cowie, 125), and instead see these films as engaging women's desires for social and sexual power. On the other hand, however, there are problems with the view of the "femme fatale" as inexorable. The fascination and excitement engendered by the "mysterious and unknowable woman" (Gledhill, 122) institutionalizes the presence of the "femme fatale" in film, which has serious consequences for readings of film noir and cultural attitudes toward female power. An overemphasis on the "femme fatale" has not only resulted in a misreading of many film noir movies, but has fed into cultural and critical obsessions with the bad, sexy woman, which inevitably become prescriptive and influence cultural discourse about female agency in counterproductive ways. In the end, the opaque powerful woman persists in objectifying female experience: the "femme fatale" is a symbol of fears about absolute female power, not a representation of complex female experience, which I see as lacking in most popular images of women, but which is often present in connection with film noir's women. *Klute*'s Bree Daniels is psychologized perhaps not as a matter of lost power (and failed transgressiveness) but as a valuing of women's lives.

There is an alternative to the inaccessibility model (the mysterious and opaque woman) for feminist criticism, which demands a fuller understanding of noir women's many-sided experience and which might pave the way for us to learn from their victimization within patriarchy, their difficult conscious and unconscious choices, and their high intelligence. Rather than promoting images of women that emphasize their spirit and unknowable power, and rather than promoting images of women that rely on their bodies, finally, we need to illustrate the contexts that inform women's experience. I want to suggest some of the reasons why we've grown accustomed to identifying film noir's "femme fatale" without examining these contexts that inform her presence in film noir, by doing just that: examining the settings—social, psychological, political, physical, and geographical—that define her experience, which is, I want strongly to suggest, a far better thing to define than "woman" herself.

This study seeks to modify the tone of feminist discussions about film noir's women by reorienting our attention to the narrative, social contexts, and mise-en-scene that show the relationship between women's powers and the limits placed on them by social rules. Both the view of the "femme fatale" as misogynist projection and the view of the "femme fatale" as opaque yet transgressive female force emphasize her status as object or symbol (as object of scorn or as the mysterious and opaque "other" that threatens to destroy the male subject). My aim is to adjust our focus on film noir and gender so that we illuminate these women's narratives rather than mystifying women as objects or images.

Because of the heavy focus feminist and non-feminist criticism has placed on the "femme fatale" figure, film criticism's and popular culture's preoccupations with the "femme fatale" have dominated discussions of film noir and have adversely affected popular debates about the representations of women and female experience. Staring at women in noir, viewers and critics fixate on the "femme fatale," a term that is less critical than hysterical and causes us to neglect a full examination of the gender politics and social psychology that undergird these films. As Helen Hanson has recently said in *Hollywood Heroines: Women in Film Noir and the Female Gothic Film*, "the 'femme fatale' has cast an imaginative shadow over the period" (14). Hanson's reorientation of our attention to female subjectivity introduces a new and much-needed correction to feminist studies of film noir, focusing on narrative rather than image. What this opens up for us is a way of conceiving of representations of women in film noir which more precisely accounts for the social psychology introduced in these films. This study seeks to understand why critical and popular discussion of the "femme fatale" has swamped careful readings of women and gender in film and attempts to suggest a more nuanced way of reading women in noir.

There are interrelated cultural, textual, and generic problems that beset readings of noir. First, there is an internalized preoccupation on the part of viewers and critics with role modeling as the foundation for feminist discussion. Such narrow understanding of what is feminist—characters who are recognizably activist, who model behavior that we imagine might empower women in the "real world"—short-circuits attention to the patriarchal social scripts presented in film noir. In other words, a female character may not in herself be feminist, but her story may be. A good example might be Louise Brooks as Lulu in *Pandora's Box* (1929), who is systematically read by viewers seduced by the film's title in terms of the mythifying image of Pandora, which keeps us from sufficiently articulating the sources of Lulu's tragedy: a social script written by patriarchy that Lulu is unaware of; a social psychology that does not allow Lulu to pursue her desires without punishment. Instead of reading Lulu we gaze at her and mark her as destructive, as "femme fatale."

What happens to Lulu happens to others. A recent book review by Manohla Dargis, film reviewer for *The New York Times*, invokes typical stereotypes of women in film. Days after calling attention to the limited female presence in the very best American films made recently (in a glowing review of Paul Thomas Anderson's *There Will Be Blood* [2007]), Dargis reviewed Jeanine Basinger's *The Star Machine* (2007), taking

Basinger to task for her romantic view of the Hollywood star system. Dargis demystifies Basinger's sentimental recounting of Hollywood's classic stars, such as Lana Turner, but recasts Turner in analogously mystifying terms, calling her, in reference to Cora Smith in *The Postman Always Rings Twice* (1946), a "poisonous honey pot": "[Lana Turner] plays a slutty goddess in [*The Postman Always Rings Twice*], a poisonous honey pot, and all she has to do is look lovely and sexually available, which she does by gently parting her pretty plum lips ... you don't believe a word she says. She's a beautiful lie." Despite the nice phrasing of the last sentence, the reading does more for enhancing ideation surrounding the "femme fatale" figure than it does for glossing the film, which, in my view, presents a more complicated role in Cora Smith than this language allows for, a particular point I'll revisit in Chapter 2. In her review of *There Will Be Blood*, Dargis says in a significant aside, "(Like most of the finest American directors working now, Mr. Anderson makes little on-screen time for women.)." There is, as Dargis notes, scant attention paid to women in the great-American film about "the failure story," Orson Welles's description of the subject of *Citizen Kane* when Welles discussed whether or not the film was based on the life of William Randolph Hearst (Mulvey, *Citizen Kane*, 80). Complicated narrative for women commands little attention, as compared with representations of failed men (American icons such as Hearst or Scorsese's Jake LaMotta) because of the cultural dominance of gender myths surrounding the idea of female agency. The mystification of women as "poisonous honeypot[s]" is one example of why we don't tend to engage a more detailed and nuanced reading not only of female characters but of the narrative contexts (reflecting social realities) that inform and in some cases determine their choices. Film viewers and film critics and scholars make judgments about the appropriateness of representations based on role modeling and already established images of women that are canonized. We look for ameliorative models of feminist representation. If the characters don't optimistically role model for viewers, the representation fails as a feminist narrative.

This is exemplified by Diane Waldman in her review of *Positive Images* in Patricia Erens's edited volume, *Issues in Feminist Film Criticism* (1991). For Waldman, *Positive Images*, an interdisciplinary catalogue of texts about sex roles, offers a limited idea of what "positive images" might mean. Waldman cites instances in which Artel and Wengraf (the authors of the catalog) invoke narrow criteria for making judgments. One example is the catalog's entry on a feminist film about a woman, "Janie Sue," who lives on a farm but doesn't "succeed": "The authors seem to fault the film for leaving us with a sense of struggle or process instead of supplying the inevitable 'happy ending'" (15). Such resistance to complex representations of female experience, seen as falling short because they don't represent female success (defined very narrowly) or as anti-feminist because they show women unable to transcend the social and cultural forces that limit or oppress them, leaves little room for compelling discussions about female agency and its relationship to society and culture.[3] As Andrew Britton has said in his discussion of women in noir:

> It is not necessary to formulate "positive images" of female strength, resistance or independence in order to produce a narrative that criticizes patriarchy from a woman's point of view, and many works of the greatest dramatic and ideological power have chosen instead to represent the tragic waste or perversion of a woman's struggle for autonomy and self-definition in the context of an implacably hostile and oppressive culture.
>
> (214)

In keeping with this lack of rigor in examining the variety of contexts in which images of women and female experience can be read, we complacently absorb the images of women that seem to conform to the familiar types, such as the "femme fatale," that hold sway in our mental landscape—Turner's "poisonous honeypot."

The mythifying social gaze we direct at women can be seen in very different kinds of cases, in examples of women seeking position and power who don't neatly fall into readily available categories, such as Hillary Clinton; and in examples of women whose actions readily call forth familiar language that codifies their meaning in the culture. The latter can be seen in the surprising language used (primarily by the Italian press) to describe the "character" of Amanda Knox, the Seattlite accused in 2007 of murdering a British student while studying abroad in Perugia: Knox, with her "icy blue eyes" (Fisher, *NYT*, November 13, 2007), was said to be a "Manhunter, insatiable in bed." "She lives," Italy's daily paper *Corriere della Sera* declaimed, "only for pleasure." Amanda Knox either killed the poor woman, or she did not, but the language of the "femme fatale" seems remarkably accessible as a way for the media to package her as a source of excitement and lurid entertainment. Carla Bruni, too, has drawn media attention for her reputation as "Maneater." That the label spans across circumstances ranging from college students accused of murder to ex-models who believe in polygamy suggests the extent to which such language infects our way of talking about female agency more generally, a point the misogyny unearthed by Hillary Clinton's presidential candidacy surely demonstrates.

The volcanic commentary on Clinton dehumanizes her and at the same time mythifies her as something Other that must be contained, as is demonstrated in the writing on a T-shirt promoted by a popular website: "Life's a bitch, why vote for one? Anti-Hillary '08." American political culture (versus popular culture) shares, to some extent, the misogyny directed at Hillary Clinton. Unable to abide the fact that Clinton doesn't conform to the stereotypes the culture comfortably projects onto women (domestic and maternal or sexual), Clinton-haters attack her on both grounds, such as in the Facebook group, "Hillary Clinton: Stop Running for President and Make Me a Sandwich," or another, "Hillary for President. She Puts the C—in Country." About the Internet fervor surrounding Clinton, C. J. Pascoe, a research sociologist with the Digital Youth Project at Berkeley's Institute for the Study of Social Change, says, "the broader society ignores the implications of the conversations being conducted on these sites at its peril" (qtd. in Tilove). Attempts to contain Clinton's influence reflect, as Pascoe suggests, a "feminist icon who stokes male insecurities about changing gender relations."[4]

Clinton's history of violating the conventional role of "wife"—first wife, first lady—established her as a New Woman, a transgressor, in cultural discourse in the 1990s. In 1992, she claimed on CBS's *Sixty Minutes* that "I am not sitting here as some little woman standing by my man, like Tammy Wynette," and professed that same year that she "could have stayed home and baked cookies and had teas," but instead pursued her professional ambitions and entered public life.[5] During the presidential primary campaign, Clinton was called shrill by MSNBC, the network that also compared her "look" at Obama during one of the debates as "the look, the look toward [Obama], looking like everyone's first wife standing outside a probate court" (Seelye and Bosman, *NYT*, June 13, 2008). Indeed, like popular commentary surrounding the New Woman—see the sketch of the "tigress" New Woman in Conrad's 1895 sketch in Figure 0.1[6]—and the women in noir, the intense ideation surrounding Hillary Clinton reflects the resurgence of misogynist discourse during times that provoke gender distress: late-Victorian feminisms; post-World War II shifts in gender roles ("the dislocation," as Krutnik nicely puts it, "of men from their former sense of being the prime movers of culture" [64]); and the prospect of a woman "leading the free world." Following Clinton's "non-concession speech" on June 3, 2008,

Figure 0.1   Conrad sketch, ca. 1895. Lilly Library, Bloomington, Indiana.

The Guardian's Michael Tomasky raged that Clinton's speech was "emasculating."[7] Specific appropriation of the idea of the "femme fatale" in connection with Clinton may be seen in Chris Matthews's reference to her as a "she-devil" (Seelye and Bosman, *NYT*, June 13, 2008), but is best reflected in similarly overdetermined remarks made by journalist and former speech-writer Peggy Noonan, who says about coverage of Hillary Clinton:

> Deep down journalists think she's a political Rasputin who will not be dispatched. Prince Yusupov served him cupcakes laced with cyanide, emptied a revolver, clubbed him, tied him up and threw him in a frozen river. When he floated to the surface they found he'd tried to claw his way from under the ice. That is how reporters see Hillary. And that is a grim and over-the-top analogy, which I must withdraw. What I really mean is they see her as the Glenn Close character in "Fatal Attraction": "I won't be ignored, Dan!"
>
> (Noonan, 2008)

NPR's Ken Rudin also compared Clinton with Glenn Close's character in *Fatal Attraction*—"She's going to keep coming back, and they're not going to stop her" (Seelye and Bosman, *NYT*, June 13, 2008). In a discussion of the relative bias of *The New York Times*'s coverage of Clinton, Clark Hoyt, the "Public Editor," observed particularly the vituperative attacks on Clinton in the editorials of Maureen Dowd, the "relentless nature of [Dowd's] gender-laden assault on Clinton." Hoyt noted

Dowd's invocation of a "femme fatale" figure in her "language painting [Clinton] as a 50-foot woman with a suffocating embrace, a conniving film noir dame."[8] In the same way, such entrenched cultural ideation about female power makes it hard for viewers to respond to films that present nuanced portraits of women without branding them either as, or in relation to, the "femme fatale" figure.

Another problem that obstructs our critical understanding of women in noir is based on textual misapprehension: the privileging of gazing at images rather than reading narrative in film, a natural consequence of film scholars' social and theoretical orientation to film. Greater attention to mise-en-scene, narrative, and context, I want to suggest, serves feminist understanding of women in noir more fully, since, first, the ways in which these films contextualize female independence and desire (classically marked as the workings of the "femme fatale") illuminate the subversiveness of the representation of gender in film noir and, second, the shift from focusing on woman as image may help to sharpen reading practices that have been obscured by the mystifying gaze at the "femme fatale."

Excessive attention to the "femme fatale" has functioned, in exclusionary ways. Steve Neale observes that a narrow conception of genres results in flawed judgment when it comes to reading films and film history. So too, I want to suggest, does a narrow focus on the "femme fatale" figure close off fuller discussion and understanding of the multidimensional representation of women in noir:

> The problem—or at any rate the problem for *noir's* proponents—is that the systematic application of many of the criteria they have advanced as definitive tend either to necessitate the exclusion or marginalization of films and genres generally considered as central, or else necessitate the inclusion of films and genres generally considered as marginal. This in turn has knock-on effects for those who ascribe a socio-historical significance to *noir*, or who wish to explain and interpret its ideological features and functions.
>
> (Neale, 153)

As Neale observes, canonical noir attributes (such as the "femme fatale") appear in films linked to other genres; these features, I want to add, take on a different tone when related to other genres, as in the "woman's picture," as I'll discuss throughout this study in connection with "marginal noir," such as *Whirlpool* (1949), *The Damned Don't Cry* (1950), and *Crime of Passion* (1957). At the same time, many films canonically noted for their inclusion of the "femme fatale" are deeply interested in the portrayal of female desire, ambition, and victimization in culture and society. Neale's work is important in its prodding us to reimagine genre in more flexible terms to attain better clarity about film history and the social and ideological work done in and by Hollywood film. Although Neale is here discussing film noir as genre, I think the point about applying categories narrowly can be usefully applied to our treatment of the "femme fatale." Analogously to the way that Neale is concerned about the arbitrary construction of film noir as a genre, the category of the "femme fatale" "tends to homogenize" the role of women in 1940s and 1950s Hollywood film (3).

One of the concerns guiding this project is that generally in film studies, what has been lost to some extent in the drive for theoretical rigor is sufficient attention to nuance and complexity in tone and narrative. A rich analysis of film may be further compromised, as suggested above, when films under investigation are defined in strict generic terms, adding another layer of theoretical apparatus. As film scholarship in the 1970s strove for relevance, it focused increasingly on defining cinematic structure, on making universal theoretical claims that justified a practice of sustained academic inquiry. Over time, this has resulted in an erosion of close readings; often, a dull level of generality presiding in discussions of the tone, narrative, and meaning of individual films.

I hope to model in the chapters that follow a critical analysis of film noir that might help to revitalize close readings in film studies, but that also explores the role of film noir in producing, sometimes in conserving, and, as I believe is very often the case in the best readings of film noir, in changing and revising cultural norms. While Philip Kemp is certainly right when he says that "film noir can be seen as a riposte, a sour, disenchanted flip side to the brittle optimism and flag-waving piety of much of Hollywood's 'official' output of the period" (86), I believe that the searing tone of film noir carries with it an ethical force, a kind of activism that I think Sylvia Harvey alludes to when she discusses the "absent family in film noir" in Kaplan's *Women in Film Noir*:

> The absence or disfigurement of the family both calls attention to its own lack and to its own deformity, and may be seen to encourage the consideration of alternative institutions for the reproduction of social life. Despite the ritual punishment of acts of transgression, the vitality with which these acts are endowed produces an excess of meaning which cannot finally be contained. Narrative resolutions cannot recuperate their subversive significance.
>
> (Kaplan, 1978, 33)

It isn't just the "subversive significance" of noir that constitutes what I am suggesting is the ethics of noir. The ethics of film noir lies, as I'll discuss more fully in Chapter 5, in its rich modernist representation of human loss; its portraits of social alienation; its analysis of the cultural game-changers that have particular and acute consequences for women; and its registers of failures of communication and longing for meaningful activity. In poetic and expressive language and image, film noir confronts the vacancies of human experience in a psychosocial world. Such confrontation is less "sour," in Kemp's words, than tough, provocative, and, finally, socially constructive, rather than apolitical or pessimistic.

In "A Brief Essay on Optimism," by Pierre Kast, a piece that originally appeared in *Positif* in 1953, Kast responds to an essay by Kanapa which

> clarifies and sums up a campaign, which has been going on for several years now, against the "morbid" and the "pessimistic" and the "apolitical" in the cinema, a campaign fought on two fronts: an intense search for anything smacking of decadence in films as well as a fanfare to celebrate whatever they contain of an optimistic nature.
>
> (Palmer, 44).

Kast argues against the prevailing notion that movies about despair threaten the culture and film art. Kast's essay looks forward to Frederic Jameson's idea that a film that reinstates bourgeois values comforts those who wish to maintain the status quo.

> [it] reassures the spectator, puts him to sleep, persuades him of the objective existence of the optimistic ideas therein expressed, proves to him the legitimacy and the endurance of the established order, which he rejoins exiting the theater.
>
> (Kast, in Palmer, 46)

Kast focuses his remarks on film noir a little later in this short essay:

> Now it seems the noir detective film, a genre that suffered historical liquidation, should be for the theorists of optimism one of the great enemies of the cinema, whereas the genre's liquidation itself is incredibly meaningful. It is not only that William Wyler has gone from *The Best Years of Our Lives* to *Detective Story*, but even the subject itself of *All the King's Men* has been redone from an optimistic point

of view by Gerald Mayer, a new director, former official employee of
the MPAA in Europe, in his film *Sellout* (1951).

(Palmer, 48)

Kast argues an important position, that film should unsettle viewers and
upset prevailing views. Given film noir's abiding interest in offering up
the contradictions of human experience in society, Kast's quotation of
Engels is apt:

> The novelist perfectly fulfills his function, when through a faithful
> representation of existing social relations, he destroys conventional
> illusions about the nature of those relations, shakes up the optimism
> of the bourgeois world, forcing it to doubt the endurance of the exist-
> ing order, even if he does not indicate a solution, even if he does not,
> in any obvious way, take sides.

(qtd. in Kast; Palmer, 49).

Film noir performs this function, casting uncertainty and prodding
reflection on the instability of psychosocial relations.

More recently, in his chapter on "Politics and Censorship" in *More Than
Night: Film Noir in its Contexts*, James Naremore identifies Paul Schrader
as well as Alain Silver and Elizabeth Ward (by way of their entries in
Film Noir: An Encyclopedic Reference to the American Style) as examples of
those putting forth the view of noir as apolitical and existentially dark
(103). Naremore later in this chapter distinguishes between the "cynicism and misanthropy" of one strain of noir, mentioning Hitchcock
and Wilder, and the socially activist films of Welles and Huston, lean-
ing toward "humanism and political engagement" (125). In my mind,
Paul Schrader, whose film credits across the decades include *Taxi Driver*
(1976) and *Raging Bull* (1980) (screenwriter), as well as *Affliction* (1997)
(director), doth protest too much. The rich and fascinating focus in
his films on gender psychosis constitutes their important contribution
to the history of film noir. Then, too, while I understand Naremore's
observation concerning the cynicism of Hitchcock's and Wilder's view of
humankind, many of Hitchcock's and Wilder's films, as I hope to show
in this book, depict the traumas of gender ideation and represent with
sympathy the failures of men and women to thrive in society. Such traumas speak directly to the haunting modern and contemporary stories of
loss, privation, and desire that film noir seeks to illuminate.

Film noir reflects changes in sociocultural conditions, just as other
texts signal what is happening in society and culture and the

transformations in attitudes toward gender from one historical period to the next. In Chapter 4, I coin the term *Victorinoir* to account for Victorian literature's dark and apprehensive representations of modern transitions in social relations. In this chapter, I focus mainly on proto-noir anxieties about female empowerment in late nineteenth-century literature. *Victorinoir* poet/novelist Thomas Hardy prefigured the tone of film noir, however, as well as some of its narrative patterns, when he said in "In Tenebris II," "if way to the Better there be, it exacts a full look at the Worst" (l. 14). In some ways, Hardy's line evokes the "femme fatale," since we can, I believe, garner a "better" understanding of the psychosocial expectations that compose the idea of the "femme fatale" by taking a "full look" at the counterproductive effects of maintaining the centrality of this concept.

Few critics and viewers see film noir as earnest at its core. And yet, I believe that, as critics and viewers, we are ready for a close-up on the psychosocial worlds presented in film noir. We need to look more closely to see beyond superficial appearance and examine what the mirror casts back, in all its complexity. We might then move past a surface cynicism to find not only (in Kent Jones's words about Edgar Ulmer's 1945 *Detour*) "the ultimate corrective to Hollywood gloss" (qtd. in Isenberg, 21), but also a deeply affecting mode of engaging the difficulties of humans in society.

******

This project is organized into two parts. Part I, comprised of Chapters 1, 2, and 3, undertakes a general discussion of misread women in original-cycle film noir. Chapter 1 attempts to reorient our attention to film noir's women in terms of sympathy and argues generally that the presence of the "femme fatale" in film noir is drastically overstated. The analysis in this chapter focuses on close readings of major and marginal film noir, attempting not only to suggest the vastness of interest these films show in the richness of female experience and the poverty of their opportunities, but also to explore the intermittent arbitrariness of generic typing of these films that often translates into generic typing of the women within them (good girl/bad girl).

Chapter 2 will revisit the general subject of misunderstood women in noir, but with an accent on the critical frames and diagetical and extra-textual misprisions that have contributed to cultural obsessions with the "femme fatale." This chapter will demonstrate the process by which misunderstood women in noir are categorized as "femmes fatales" by the men whom they encounter, who project fantasies onto women with disastrous results. For many of these men, and in most classic film noir, men's solipsistic projections onto women—men reading women as "femmes fatales" when they are not—result in trauma and often death. Chapter 2 also suggests the extratextual repetitions of "femme fatale" ideation, projections that film critics make onto the women in noir that serve to further canonize the "femme fatale" figure.

Chapter 3 will address film noir's "mad" women: the women allied with or characterized as the "femme fatale" figure who have personality disorders. The "crazy" women I address in this chapter, Ellen Berent in *Leave Her to Heaven* (1945), Louise Howell in *Possessed* (1947), Ann Sutton in *Whirlpool* (1949), and Annie Laurie in *Gun Crazy* (1950), are all victims of gender bias, or their stories reflect the consequences of severe cultural limitations placed on women. The films themselves, all made within a five-year period immediately following the conclusion of World War II, delineate the contexts for these women's actions and behavior. Their mental illnesses are a result of the lack of affirmation and validation women are portrayed as receiving in society, and their status as murderesses and "femmes fatales" must be reoriented to a wider discussion of the sympathies they elicit and the men and social institutions that are defined in these films as unresponsive to their needs, unreceptive to their powers, and uninterested in their desires.

Part II looks backward to Victorian narrative and forward to a contemporary film, David Lynch's *Mulholland Drive* (2001), to suggest the persistency of problematic cultural attitudes toward female agency, and the continual resurgence of representation grappling with anxiety about female agency during times of change in gender identities. I argue that there are important parallels between Victorian representations of gender and film noir's expression of gender anxiety. These repetitions in the representation of female power, as well as continual misreadings of such representations, strongly suggest the resurgence of backlash in understanding female ambition and empowerment during times of social change and female advancement. Such recurrence in image and narrative patterns also reflects strong continuities in the artistic and aesthetic treatment of women and gender. The end of Part II, my analysis of *Mulholland Drive*, offers an instance of deconstructing the backlash and backward glance of gender politics and instead suggests a nuanced means of imagining female agency in the context of openness, vitality, and receptivity.

More specifically, in Part II, Chapter 4 explores parallels to film noir's representation of gender in Victorian fiction, which can usefully serve as a kind of prehistory for film noir, since the negotiations and anxieties about female power and agency so crucial to these films are prefigured in late nineteenth-century *Victorinoir* representations of women and gender. This chapter will also suggest a transition and historical link between late-Victorian narrative and film noir in silent film's so-called vamp figure, a Janus-faced female agent, evoking the cultural language of the Victorian vampire to mask the social concerns of women seeking independence and autonomy. Just as I argue that readings of women in noir need to take fuller account of the contexts delineated in and by the films that help us to explicate female experience, so too do we need to situate film noir in a broader history of representations of women that gives us insight into the relationship between text and context, and film and gender roles in society. An analysis of the cultural reemergence of strong victimized women read as "femmes fatales" in literature and film reveals a distinct relationship between moments of backlash against female social advances and cultural resistance on the part of women attempting to better position themselves. These transformations and repetitions in representation of the *femmes modernes* can help us to recognize these patterns and examine how they are received in contemporary culture.

Chapter 5 tries to reimagine the "femme fatale" figure as a tool for understanding gender and culture rather than as a fixed object of investigation and fascination. *Mulholland Drive* (2001), David Lynch's noir film about Hollywood, I will argue, alludes to the misreading of women in noir while it deconstructs that process. Referencing *Sunset Boulevard* (1950) in its self-consciousness about genre and the victimization of women in Hollywood, Lynch's film provides a more nuanced, deeply affective reorientation to representations of female experience. *Mulholland Drive* models in its perceptive contemporary reception of the "femme fatale" figure a more constructive use of the "femme fatale" as a critical tool for understanding gender and culture.

This study aims to pursue models of textual interpretation that see women in noir as victimized by hyper-masculinized men and as attempting to break free of victimization and redefine the terms of living within patriarchy. The cynical noir style is appropriate not only, as is canonically noted, to attend to the angst of the hard-boiled male protagonist, but also to tell women's stories, which can be characterized as traumatic and tragic. These stories need to be foregrounded and understood more fully as the central concern of the films.

In an essay that posits film noir's "femme fatale" as a modern tragic figure, Elizabeth Bronfen discusses the noir hero's misrecognition of the "femme fatale's" claim to tragic subjectivity. Bronfen addresses film noir's viewers and critics, who

> read the femme fatale either as an embodiment of threat or as a textual enigma and, in so doing, avoid actually seeing her as separate not only from the fantasies of the noir hero, but also from any critical preconceptions informing one's reading of a given text.
>
> (114)

Bronfen takes as her subject Phyllis Dietrichson, one of the very few (I would argue) "pure" "femmes fatales" in film noir, thus reinforcing our critical tendency to equate the unequivocally dangerous women in noir with all of the complicated female characters in these films. However, the appeal to readers to "recognize her as a separate human being, exceeding [Neff's] appropriation of her and, in so doing, exhibiting an agency of her own" moves us in an interesting and productive feminist direction, I believe, since it suggests avenues for reimagining female presence in film noir as meaningful and as multifaceted. "What would it mean," asks Bronfen,

> for us to put a stop to the series of turnings away which revolve around the "femme fatale," to abdicate the gesture of fetishism, which supports the refusal to see her as a separate human being and the refusal to accept her difference?
>
> (114)

It would mean, I submit in this project, a more sustainable freedom for women, since such freedom rests with understanding female experience, in all of its variety, complexity, struggle, and vitality, that expresses itself in so many unique ways at different times in women's lives, in film, fiction, and reality.

Part I Rereading Film Noir

1

Film Noir's "Femmes Fatales": Moving Beyond Gender Fantasies

In her essay "Professions for Women," Virginia Woolf says, "It is far harder to kill a phantom than a reality" (1988). Nowhere is this insight truer than in the culture's preoccupation with the "femme fatale," a figure I want to identify as a phantom, an illusion and myth that I wish not so much to kill, but to deconstruct as a category that feeds cultural gender fantasies. Feminist film critics have long recognized the ideological power of the "femme fatale": first in terms of her role as a projection of male fear and desire; later, as a politically forceful symbol of unencumbered power. I want not only to extend emphases by critics such as Christine Gledhill, Elizabeth Cowie, and Jans Wager on how noir speaks to women but also to show the striking extent to which "femmes fatales"—seductresses whose desires and malevolence are seemingly unmotivated—don't in fact exist in the noir movies in which so-called bad women appear.

Film noir's lead female characters predominantly demonstrate complex psychological and social identity, resisting the spectator's habit (traced in criticism and cultural responses) of seeing past her by treating her as opaque (thus a screen on which to project male fears and desires) or of fixing on her as a thing, a dangerous body, to be labeled and tamed by social roles and institutions.

This chapter will point to the dearth of film noir's actual "femmes fatales," evil women whose raison d'etre is to murder and deceive, focusing instead on films in which the "femme fatale" is presented in terms of exigency. That is, I want to call attention to the *many* female characters in original-cycle noir who are shown to be limited by, even trapped in, social worlds presented as psychotically gendered. Exigency for most so-called femmes fatales moves these women to express—in aggressive physical and verbal gestures—an insistence on independence, which is then misread as the mark of the "femme fatale." Readings of and references to the "femme fatale" miss the extent to which her role depends on the theme of female independence, often misconceiving her motives and serving mainly to confound our understanding of the gender fantasies that surround these so-called bad women. Such myths are perpetuated now both by film criticism and popular culture.

Indeed, critics have settled in their discussion of women in noir on the few female characters who conform to the notion of the quintessential "femme fatale" (as she is represented by Phyllis Dietrichson [*Double Indemnity*, 1944], Kathie Moffett [*Out of the Past*, 1947], and Brigid O'Shaughnessy [*The Maltese Falcon*, 1941]), who then define the category. This has two significant consequences: first, these few really bad women draw all of the attention; second the construction of a false binary opposition between "femmes fatales" and other women means that the large majority of female characters in noir whose roles are inflected (multifaceted and interesting) are placed into the category of "femme fatale" without close attention paid to the complexity of the character. Steve Neale argues against the exclusivity of genre conception—for example, the gangster picture being defined in terms of "a series which seems to consist, as usual, of just three films, *Little Caesar*, *The Public Enemy*, and *Scarface*" (78). So too the "femme fatale" figure is constructed around several characters who then define and, I would argue, prescribe, the role.

Such is certainly the case with Cora Smith (Lana Turner) in *The Postman Always Rings Twice* (1946). Cora is hailed as one of the central film noir "femmes fatales," but the film's presentation of her is considerably more complicated than is allowed by the label. With Phyllis Dietrichson, Cora was recently dubbed "two of the [("femme fatale"'s] most powerful screen incarnations" (Spicer, 91), and yet Cora is shown by the film to be desperately confined. This is represented most forcefully in the scene in which Nick tells her that she will be moving to Northern Canada to take care of a half-paralyzed sister of Nick's. All of Cora's hopes to "be somebody" are dashed. She's trapped. Certainly this is an important part of Cora's story. Her subjectivity, powerfully emphasized as she walks, stunned and defeated, up the stairs after the scene just alluded to, is utterly elided, however, by insisting on her being a "femme fatale."[1]

Critics and critical history have selected for the "femme fatale" and canonized these women. Current critics and popular culture have then inherited a tradition that they don't really question but rather assume: Bad women are "femmes fatales" and there will be a "femme fatale" in film noir movies. The inflexibility of the category of the "femme fatale," despite feminist attempts to problematize and complicate the label and its various contexts, leads viewers typically to take a "Where's Waldo" approach to the "femme fatale": "She's not a real 'femme fatale!'"; "She didn't kill anyone"; or "She's not very attractive." Such exclusivity in understanding the "femme fatale" stalls discussion of the complexity of her represented experience, which almost always involves a woman trapped by the narrow categories on offer for understanding female social and sexual lives.

Many film noir movies lend subjectivity to the independent women called femmes fatales, depicting the psychological motives for becoming, or acting the role of, the "femme fatale." While these motives are often clearly linked to the social conditions of women in postwar America, the depiction of "femmes fatales" frequently attributes an "inner life" to these women which allows us to read them as sympathetic characters; these films depict "femmes fatales" as inevitably growing out of repressive social milieus. As actress Lizabeth Scott, best known for her noir performances such as in *The Strange Love of Martha Ivers* (1946), *Dead Reckoning* (1947), and *Pitfall* (1948), has said,

> the *femme fatale* . . . was always the person, in most of the films that I did, who had the greatest understanding. She knew life better than most females of the era. She knew that life could be good and life could be bad, she knew what was right and she knew what was wrong, but . . . there were certain things she had to do.
>
> (*Noir Reader* 3, 195)

Samuel Fuller echoes Scott's remarks when he talks about the blindness and hypocrisies surrounding perceptions of Kelly, the sympathetic prostitute in Fuller's *The Naked Kiss* (1964): "When [the townspeople] find out about her past, everybody assumes she's guilty as hell." "You do what you do," Fuller adds, "out of necessity" (*Noir Reader* 3, 48).[2] Fuller points up the two-pronged difficulty for women represented in film noir. To preserve itself, patriarchal culture projects images onto women that perpetuate a binary opposition of good girl versus "femme fatale." Attempts to assert independent existence and to live beyond or to escape such projected gender fantasies then upset patriarchal order and cause it to redouble its efforts to categorize these women as deviant.

This process of projection, female resistance and assertion of subjectivity, and patriarchal reinforcement is fully demonstrated in Edgar Ulmer's *Detour* (1945), particularly in the representation of the film's most compelling female character, Vera, played by Ann Savage.

As James Naremore says, "ruthlessly hard and half-crazed," Vera "makes every "femme fatale" in the period look genteel by comparison" (149). Tania Modleski has called Vera "one of the most ferocious persecutory *femmes fatales* in the history of cinema" (qtd in Isenberg, 62). However, *Detour*, reflecting on modern ambivalence toward empowered women, offers a commentary on the construction of woman in terms of bifurcated images of good and evil. For example, the protagonist Al Roberts (Tom Neal) says in a voiceover, as he looks at a profile of Vera:

> I got the impression of beauty: not the beauty of a movie actress, mind you, or the beauty you dream about when you're with your wife, but a natural beauty, a beauty that's almost homely because it's so real. . . . Then suddenly she turned to face me.

The shock of recognition deflates high-grounded solipsistic projections about women. As in Mark McPherson's struggle in Otto Preminger's *Laura* (1944) to translate his obsession with the image of Laura into mastery of the woman herself; as in Scotty Ferguson's desperate struggle in *Vertigo* (1958) to maintain his ideation of Madeleine in the face of the real Judy Barton, in this scene in *Detour*, the "folksy" portrait of Vera gives way to a disappointing and threatening reality: "Then suddenly, she turned to face me." The film *Detour*'s concern with the ideal versus the real, leaving out the complexity of the actual experiences of individuals that inform or complicate their gender roles, is also emphasized in Al's later voiceover:

> If this were fiction, I would fall in love with Vera, marry her and make a respectable woman of her. Or else she'd make some supreme class-A sacrifice for me and die. Sue and I would bawl a little over her grave and make some crack about there's good in all of us. But Vera unfortunately was just as rotten in the morning as she'd been the night before.

This overdetermined presentation of fictional positions on women, all of which deny her complex identity which might allow for empowered subjecthood, help to explain Vera's shrill demand to be seen for who she is. Like other honest vamps (one thinks even of the most fatal of femmes, *Out of the Past*'s Kathie Moffett, who says to Jeff Markham, "I never pretended to be anything but what I was. You just didn't see it. That's why I left you"), Vera is motivated by exigency.

As Andrew Britton says, for Vera, dying of consumption, "every word and action is designed to convince Al that she can do exactly what she likes with him ('I'm not through with you by a long shot!')" (179). Later, Vera says of the plan to steal Haskell's inheritance, "For that kind of dough, I'd let you cut my leg off." As the desperation of this remark suggests, I think Naremore is right when he notes that while Vera is "sullen" and "dangerous," she's also a "sympathetic figure" (149). This strangely mixed treatment of Vera is apparent in her language, "cracking like a whip," as Britton says, full of a desperate desire to claim agency in a culture that habitually denies women their subjectivity. While in simple generic terms Vera is an absolutely unambiguous "femme fatale," the nature of her presence in the film is more complex than is allowed by simply referencing her as the film's "femme fatale."

Because the yoking together of sexuality, evil, and powerful women seems to me an insufficiently addressed habit in viewing film noir, I want to propose a modified perspective that builds on the work of feminists who suggest that female viewers find grounds for empathy in understanding the "femme fatale." For fully engaged readings of film noir, I will argue, need to confront the simulacral fantasies that not only surround the "femme fatale" but that generate ideas in the culture that have very material effects. By shifting our nomenclature, for example, to talk about these trapped women as "hard-boiled females," or, simply, modern women, *femmes modernes*, rather than strictly as "femmes fatales," we can see more clearly the ongoing force of binary oppositions in the presentation of gender in contemporary culture and we highlight film noir's aim to destabilize gender categories.

The predominance of the idea of the "femme fatale," I've been suggesting, profoundly shapes our viewing of all women in film noir. This keeps us from recognizing not only the complex levels of female subjectivity but also the extent to which women are trapped in social roles they can't change, or how they are trapped particularly into performing the role of "femme fatale" that then perpetuates ideation surrounding these women. Says cynical Dev to Alicia in *Notorious*, "Dry your eyes, baby; it's out of character." These traps, prefigured in late-Victorian narrative, as I will argue in Chapter 4, most often take the form of simple opposition and dichotomy.

Such is the case in Fritz Lang's *The Big Heat* (1953), in which the inspiring wife, Katie Bannion, is destroyed by the Lagana underworld and the criminal taint of the city, the public realm. In introducing his BFI book on *The Big Heat*, Colin McArthur comments on the starkness of the difference in tone between Dave Bannion's life at home (Figure 1.1) and his visit to "The Retreat," the seedy bar in which he finds Lucy Chapman (Figure 1.2). McArthur juxtaposes stills of these

Figure 1.1   Domestic Bliss: Jocelyn Brando and Glenn Ford as Katie and Dave Bannion in *The Big Heat* (BFI), © 1953, renewed 1981 Columbia Pictures Industries, Inc. All rights reserved. Courtesy of Columbia Pictures.

Figure 1.2   Lucy Chapman (Dorothy Green) and Bannion at "The Retreat," *The Big Heat* (BFI), © 1953, renewed 1981 Columbia Pictures Industries, Inc. All rights reserved. Courtesy of Columbia Pictures.

opposite worlds (the caption reads "Counterpoint: 'the bright friendly world of Bannion home . . . ' '. . . and the bleak world of The Retreat.'" [8]). When Dave Bannion leaves the comfort of domestic contentment to follow a lead on Duncan's death, the radical shift in Bannion's affect can be seen as the character, played by Glenn Ford, dons his hat. The film abruptly shifts its attention from Dave's domestic banter with his wife Katie—"Tha's good steak"—to Bannion's detached suspicious detective-speak in the bar—"Lucy Chapman here?"

In the interview that follows, Bannion shows contempt for Lucy: he reads her categorically as "femme fatale" because she works at "The Retreat" and because she has been involved in adultery with Duncan, one of Bannion's detective colleagues who has just committed suicide. Bannion, like most noir protagonists, has only two categories for women, perfect wives and corrupt women on the take. He mistakenly places Lucy in the latter category and by misreading her motives and character contributes to events that lead to her brutal murder. Bannion thus stands in for the unwitting film noir viewer who repeats this pattern almost obsessively by ignoring the often nuanced presentation of women's experience in noir.

Lang makes this point clearly when he shows Lucy's face in close-up as she reacts, wounded, to Bannon's tough-speak accusation, "What's the angle, Lucy?" Lucy says, in a broken and poignant reply, "Me?" and we are made alert to Bannion's summary blindness to her. Such failure of vision, a common theme in noir, not only looks forward to Bannion's disgusted dismissal of Debby Marsh (Gloria Grahame), thug Vince Stone's girlfriend ("I wouldn't touch anything of Vince Stone's with a ten-foot pole," says Bannion callously), but also antici-pates *Chinatown*'s Jake Gittes's naïve and at the same time brutish categorization of Evelyn Mulwray as the unambiguous betrayer. Jake's mistake in interpreting Evelyn Mulwray as a "femme fatale," and the cynical mistrust that undergirds his reading of her, contributes, of course, to events that lead to Evelyn's gruesome death and the hor-rible exploitation of her daughter/sister Katherine by the malevolent patriarch Noah Cross (John Huston).[3]

In her discussion of women in 40s films, Molly Haskell has suggested the close relation between the habit of reading women as image and the particularly dichotomous nature of these images of women:

> It is not the evil in women, but the mutual exclusiveness of good and evil that we resent, since it is a way of converting women from their ambiguous reality into metaphors, visitations of an angel or a devil.[4]

> (199)

While on the one hand Haskell's comment critiques the binaries that cause misogyny, her alternative paradigm of "ambiguity" seems problematic, since "femmes fatales" aren't really ambiguous any more than any complex human subject is ambiguous—ambiguity becomes here another virtual space ready to be filled by projected ideation. Still, Haskell's analysis is important, as she goes on to quote Barbara Stanwyck's comment on women in Preston Sturges's noir comedy *The Lady Eve*, that "the best aren't as good as you think they are, and the bad ones aren't as bad . . . not nearly as bad." In her excellent book *Fast-Talking Dames*, Maria DiBattista makes a similar point about Sturges's film:

> [T]he film allays the anxieties that it has itself aroused about the designing woman, the seductive Eve, by assuring us that Jean and Eve, the good (who isn't as good as we want) and the bad (who isn't as bad as we think) are joined in the middle distance.
>
> (323)

We might contrast this acknowledgment of the complexity of female experience with the exchange in *Out of the Past* (1947) between good-girl Ann and noir protagonist Jeff Bailey/Markham, as they discuss "femme fatale" Kathie Moffett: Ann says, "She can't be all bad—nobody's all bad," to which Jeff replies, "She comes the closest." What so many film noir texts demonstrate in contrast is the hard-boiled reality of female experience, as these so-called femmes fatales struggle to assert a power the male protagonists deny them.[5]

Through its rehearsal of binary oppositions, film noir criticizes gendered divisions of space, a strain of commentary important to look at, given contemporary culture's continuing obsession with defining social spaces as gendered (e.g. Spike TV, Super Bowl half-time shows, and the bland anodyne role modeling endorsed on Lifetime, in "chick flicks," and at Oxygen.com). Film noir has always shown the destructive nature of these boundaries by demonstrating what happens when women cross these lines: they become a severe threat to dominant male culture. Rita Hayworth's famed striptease performance of "Put the Blame on Mame" suggests the misogynist branding of women who deviate from their role as it is prescribed by cultural binary oppositions. In *Gilda*, Johnny Farrell can't abide Gilda's verbal, psychological, and sexual power over him. He reacts so violently and cruelly to her (comparing women to insects, for example) that the movie enacts in the story the annihilating process of "putting the blame on Mame." A psychotic extension of this invective against the woman for deviating from a role designed and mastered by conventional male power is seen in Cable's speech at the end of *Klute* (1971). Cable (Charles Cioffi) is here speaking to Bree Daniels, the call girl he blames for inciting him to become a murderer:

> There are little corners in everyone which were better left alone. . . . You're too warped to do anything with your life, so you prey upon the sexual fantasies of others. There are weaknesses that should never be exposed. But that's your stock in trade: a man's weakness. And I was never fully aware of mine until you brought them out.

Bree Daniels is a "femme fatale" place-holder in *Klute*; her role, as it is seen by the psychotic Cable, invites comparison with the many other victims of projections onto women in film noir, as in the case of *Taxi Driver* (1976), where the potential for absolute derangement in viewing women alternately as angel and whore is explicitly demonstrated by Travis Bickle. Travis, played by Robert De Niro, idealizes Betsy (Cybil Shepherd)—who first appears as a vision in white, as Kathie Moffett did in *Out of the Past*—only to categorically devalue her several scenes later as "just like the rest." After Betsy rejects Travis when he takes her on a date to a pornographic film, he shouts that she is "going to die in hell like the rest of them." Later in the film, Travis once again shows his inability to adopt a more complex reading of female experience when he ignores the reality of 12-year-old Iris's troubled life (as played by Jodie Foster) in order to save her from prostitution and degradation. The film shows the dramatic bifurcation in Travis's view of woman (innocent or evil) in his absurdly beatific encomium to the young prostitute as he cups her face in his hand: "Sweet Iris."[6]

Feminist film critics have recognized that male protagonists in noir hold responsibility for their fates, but this insight hasn't led viewers to see fully the implications of these observations: mainly, that the presence of the "femme fatale" in film noir movies is drastically overstated and almost exclusively the result of male projection, as may be only truly obvious in the extreme case of *Klute*, as cited above. However, film noir is ripe with suggestions that the "femme fatale" is a projection of male gender psychosis and the women labeled as "femmes fatales" are often struggling to escape this projection.

The point is exemplified in Maria Elena Buszek's discussion of the 40s pin-up "Varga Girl." During World War II, the modern woman, the American *femme moderne*, struggled with working alongside men in the public sphere, taking new note of "the power and problems that their sexuality posed in relations with their male counterparts" (215). Citing Filene's *Him/Her/Self* (163), Buszek comments that "women were often blamed for the 'distraction' they posed in the workplace and forbidden from wearing sweaters or form-fitting clothing" (216). The changing social position of women at home had implications for the female image abroad, in the instance, for example, of women who were often painted on Army bombers during World War II:

> Archival images of World War II bomber art include dozens of bombers on which Varga Girls appeared, menacingly dubbed "The Dark Angel," "Double Trouble," and "War Goddess" . . . . One bomber pilot wrote *Esquire* to testify that "the Varga beauty stenciled onto his bomber made a German pilot come within gun range for a better look."
>
> (212)

As much as film noir movies may extend sympathy toward the male crisis of identity after the destabilization of gender roles occurring in America during WWII, these films also suggest, more subversively still, the trap that society lays for women whose beauty and power are thought, as Cable's speech decries, to exploit "a man's weakness." The women labeled the "femme fatale" are the "fall guys" for men and are branded as evil, as potentially deceptive, even before they speak.

In *Laura* (directed by Otto Preminger in 1944), a movie that examines the habit of casting women as a priori "femmes fatales," Lydecker and McPherson worry throughout the film that Laura will betray her lovers. But the film presents its concern through these men's obsessive ideation, provoked, in McPherson's case quite literally, by Laura's image. The bullying Lydecker makes the point as he reveals that "the way [Laura] listened was more eloquent than speech," ratifying the idea of the good woman as the silent woman, as the image, as the portrait. "What difference," Laura says to the interrogating McPherson, "does it make what I say? You've made up your mind I'm guilty." Because McPherson has become infatuated with the portrait of Laura in this film—McPherson identifies Laura herself with the painting of her—her actual appearance disorients him into casting her as a "femme fatale" (Figure 1.3). Characterizing this disorientation, Slavoj Žižek has said, the "'real' Laura emerges as a non-symbolized fantasmatic surplus, a ghostlike apparition" (Copjec, 220).

The fantasmatic, however, threatens to be contained as Laura becomes appropriated and consumed by male desire, like the Duke's

Figure 1.3 Laura (Gene Tierney), McPherson (Dana Andrews), and the image in *Laura* © 1944 Twentieth Century Fox. All rights reserved. BFI.

wives in Robert Browning's 1842 dramatic monologue "My Last Duchess," a proleptically noir poem that critiques the Duke's projection of masculine power onto women. The poem exploits the term "object," presenting the Duke's wives as portraits/images ("That's my last Duchess painted on the wall" [l. 1]), as well as goal and possession: "his fair daughter's self . . . is my object" (ll. 52–3). The poem explains violence against women as the result of male projection, offering an interesting analogy to the representation of male protagonists in noir. Further, the poem dramatizes a moment in which a male suitor (the Duke) assumes that his auditor (the agent of his next wife's father) will make the same interpretations he does, just as, I am suggesting, the poem's readers and *Laura*'s viewers should not be sharing the perspective of the dominant male characters within the narrative. Indeed, *Laura* pushes us to make judgments on the men around Laura. As Angela Martin has pointed out, the expected role of Laura as this film's "femme fatale" is undermined by the film's insistence that Laura's mystery is entirely a result of male projection:

> Laura only expresses *anything* of the *"femme fatale"* inasmuch as that is projected through the behavior of the men around her. . . . Laura herself becomes a silent and still (painted) image during her long weekend absence, which gives the other characters limitless space

to recreate her in their own terms. . . . But it is the male characters whose shadows are thrown; it is the male characters who produce "the fatal": Laura just brings out what is already there (which is, of course, the real female crime in film noir).

(213, 214)

As in *Laura*, the introduction of woman via portrait or image is common in noir: Diane Redfern, the real murdered victim in *Laura*, is only seen in the film in a photograph; in *The Woman in the Window* (1944), Professor Wanley (Edward G. Robinson) is seduced into noir reverie by a painting of a woman he sees in a store window; our first image of Joyce Harwood in *The Blue Dahlia* (1946) is in a photograph on her husband's desk; Mona Stevens, the victimized so-called femme fatale in *Pitfall* (1948), is also first introduced to us as a photograph in a modeling portfolio. That these women appear at first as photographic or painted images strongly suggests their initial status as images coined by male desire, "derealized" in Mary Ann Doane's terms (*Femmes Fatales*, 146), in the service of male fantasy.

The logic of film noir deconstructs the dichotomies that structure these gender fantasies. I am suggesting that we take this insight further to question the elevation of the "femme fatale" that results from these projections of desire. While feminist film critics have discussed at some length the nature of these projections, we haven't sufficiently inferred from these analyses the problems with relying on the "femme fatale" as the main figure in film noir. We become passive and dependent on what we think we already know about women, which evokes a "femme fatale" before the narrative unfolds. This model of reading women is, I've been arguing, outlined in the films themselves, as is demonstrated in a scene from George Marshall's *The Blue Dahlia* (1946).

Early in *The Blue Dahlia*, Johnny Morrison (Alan Ladd) says thank you and goodbye to the at-this-point anonymous woman (later identified as Joyce Harwood, played by Veronica Lake), who has picked up this disappointed war veteran in LA and driven him from the dark, rainy city to sunny Malibu. Johnny says, "It's hard to say goodbye." Lake's character responds, "Why is it hard to say goodbye? You've never seen me before," to which Johnny replies, "Every guy's seen you. The trick is to find you." A remarkable instance of the process of transforming a woman into only an image of generalized male desire for the perfect woman, Joyce Harwood exists absolutely in Johnny's mind. A real woman couldn't ever live up to the preexisting image of Joyce as angel.

In *The Blue Dahlia*, there is thus a kind of inevitability in the fact that Johnny Morrison turns on Joyce when he discovers she is married to her estranged husband Harwood, played by Howard Da Silva. Deviating at all from Johnny's ideal image of her, Joyce Harwood becomes immediately suspect. Whereas before this discovery, Johnny has placed her on a pedestal, after the discovery, he dismisses her as "baby": "See you later, baby," he says (as he effectively abandons her), invoking by so doing a conventional verbal marker for sexualized woman. Joyce is even, late in the film, iconographically linked to Helen Morrison, who most nearly evokes the "femme fatale": on the one hand, Helen is an adulteress who drinks, smokes, has accidentally killed her baby, and dresses in gold lamee; on the other hand, before Helen is murdered, she not only leaves clues to help Johnny discover her murderer, but her explanation of her life while Johnny was away evokes a sympathetic portrait of the *femmes modernes* struggling while their husbands were at war, a portrait made more complex by Johnny's threats to "make" Helen stop drinking. When Joyce Harwood repeats Helen's earlier habit of picking petals off the blue dahlias, Joyce is symbolically linked to Helen, the film's ostensible dangerous dark woman. In being allied with Helen, Joyce joins the ranks of women brutally dismissed by those such as Harwood's sidekick, who says about women, "they're all poison sooner or later."

Nicholas Ray's *Johnny Guitar* (1954) reveals the anxiety about female power that produces such ideation. Vienna, played by Joan Crawford, demonstrates a mannishness that elicits a comment from her employee Sam (John Carradine), which is striking not only for its response to gender anxiety but for its transparency in exposing this anxiety: "Never seen a woman who was more a man: She thinks like one, acts like one, and sometimes makes me feel like I'm not." Such direct commentary would be easier to take in and understand as part of a larger interpretive pattern, if viewers weren't so focused on what they expected to see in film noir. With a more sustained habit of attending to the logic of the narrative, we see clearly these films' exposure of the ideological contradictions in the dominant culture's regulations of gender.

A critique in noir films is thus leveled at the continuing cultural reading of women as a projection of male desire or fear: as domestic muse or "femme fatale," as two-faced, like Debby Marsh, Gloria Graham's character in *The Big Heat*, whose face, after Vince Stone (Lee Marvin) scalds her with coffee, is literally bifurcated—grotesque burn scars on one side oppose perfect angelic beauty on the other. As the fallen woman, she must die, but because she sacrifices herself so that Bannion can solve the crime and avenge his wife's murder, Lang's final shot of her is of the unscarred, angelic side of her face. Although the film in this shot seems to want to choose one side (angelic female savior) over the other ("femme fatale"), what the movie has shown rather methodically are the violent, even fatal, consequences of trying to define these poles as essential, and as essentially opposed.

Film noir puts pressure on these oppositions by imagining the crossing of borders, transgressions of gender roles. Such associations force a confrontation with trauma, repressed in mainstream film and culture as socially intolerable. As Vargas says in *Touch of Evil* (1958), "All border towns bring out the worst in a country." Vargas himself is complicit in the division of realms, segregating the "real Mexico" from its borders, isolating Susie in the wrongly judged "safe" zone of the Mirador Motel, but the film itself reveals the callousness and potential destructiveness of forging and maintaining segregated psychosocial domains.

Film noir movies demonstrate the violent consequences of cultural oppositions, mainly enforced according to gender, by suggesting that the violent underbelly referred to in noir is itself caused by the culture's division of complex human experience into strictly circumscribed opposing realms. Further, noir reveals the ways in which structuring experience according to these dichotomies may result in palpable cynicism that keeps us from addressing social illnesses. An example might be the famous concluding lines of *Chinatown* (1974): "Forget it Jake. It's Chinatown." But it's not just Chinatown; it's Jake's blindness and his cynicism that keep him from believing, and believing in, Evelyn Mulwray. *Chinatown* shares *The Big Heat*'s condemnation of failures of vision. These films argue for a gray view of the world that recognizes and responds sympathetically to the complexity of human experience; the logic of their stories calls attention to these failures of vision, suggesting an alternative model of sympathetic engagement to understand film noir narrative.[7]

Other noir films, such as *Phantom Lady, The Blue Gardenia, The Damned Don't Cry*, and *The Naked Kiss* challenge viewers' expectations of strict oppositions by placing the would-be "femme fatale" in the role of subject, *femme moderne* and hard-boiled female protagonist. Following this model of gender destabilization, *The Phantom Lady* (1944), Robert Siodmek's bizarre adaptation of a Cornell Woolrich novel, introduces a male lead who is utterly emasculated: hearing that Scott's wife laughed at him, the cop says glibly, "Nothing makes a man sorer than that . . . making a patsy of you, eh?"; later in the scene, Scott begins to tear up, saying "I thought guys didn't cry." In this film, woman takes on the role of "seeker hero," as Michael Walker notes (Cameron 110–15). Carol Richman notably appropriates the male gaze in a way that unsettles Laura Mulvey's positioning of the spectator as inevitably male.[8] To intimidate him into helping her solve the murder, Carol literally stares down the bartender, to the point where he runs from her into oncoming traffic and dies. Throughout the film, Carol role-plays, demonstrating the resourcefulness, flexibility, and aggressiveness of the *femme moderne.* Despite some neat ideological closure, *Phantom Lady* suggests the subversive potential of the hard-boiled female protagonist.

The insistence on the "femme fatale" as a bad female object of fascination or investigation not only causes us, as I've been arguing, to misinterpret female roles in film noir and to perpetuate unhealthy ideation in popular culture, but also leads us to draw arbitrary borders between genres whose intersections are compelling and important, as Steve Neale's work has shown and as Janey Place has noted. An over-reliance on categorization results in the "suppression of those elements which do not 'fit', and ... exclusion of films which have strong links but equally strong differences from a particular category" (Place, 39).[9]

Conventions of genre can serve to segregate stories of women, as Elizabeth Cowie has pointed out, when she argues against the location of film noir as "male melodrama" by critics such as Maureen Turin and Frank Krutnik. Cowie favors an "[examination of] the melodrama in *film noir* in order to overturn this rigid sexual division, not to affirm it" (Copjec, 130).[10] So, too, I think that analysis of narrative similarities across genres not only models a plasticity in genre conception but also serves to break down the segregation of female stories into generic compartments. *The Damned Don't Cry* (1950) for example, is deemed melodrama, a woman's picture, but the main character shares a great many qualities with the "femme fatale," if we look at that figure from a feminist perspective. As in film noir, the ostensibly melodramatic *The Damned Don't Cry* also destabilizes gender categories, as well as genre categories, since its title screams melodrama. In fact, the film not only presents a noir hard-boiled female protagonist but also unequivocally presents the "femme fatale" as a construction of male anxiety and projection.

Echoing the beginning of the better-known Joan Crawford noir vehicle *Mildred Pierce* (1945), *The Damned Don't Cry* begins with Ethel Whitehead not only trapped in the role of oppressed mother and housewife but, more significantly, victimized by the misogynist ramblings of her father, who manages to convince her husband Roy that "You'll never do enough for her." When her son is killed, Ethel decides to follow the lead of independent male loners from Sam Spade to Shane, telling Roy, who insists that he's "done the best he could," "Well it ain't good enough." The social roles that might afford Ethel something like the power and independence available to male heroes are limited to modeling and prostitution, but Ethel insists on her right to determine her life. As she says to *her* emasculated suitor Marty Blackford: "You're a nice guy, but the world isn't for nice guys. You gotta kick and punch and belt your way up cuz nobody's going to give you a lift. You've got to do it yourself. Cuz nobody cares about us except ourselves." "The only thing that counts," says this hard-boiled *femme moderne*, "is that stuff you take to the bank, that filthy buck that everybody sneers at but slugs to get."

The desperation of Ethel Whitehead's speech notwithstanding, the language is also that of the canonic hard-boiled male protagonist ("You gotta kick and punch and belt your way up cuz nobody's going to give you a lift"). However, when a man makes this kind of speech, the myth he upholds is that of the male loner, like Chandler's detective, who minds the mean streets "a lonely man" (Chandler, qtd. in Hirsch, *The Dark Side of the Screen*, 33). We can expose the ideologically conservative cast of this gesture by simply pointing out that the male loner figure is never really alone. In fact, he's supported by a network of homosocial relations. The men work together, or at least believe in one another, like the family of men in Chandler's *The Blue Dahlia* (1946), or the existential partnering of Neff and Keyes in *Double Indemnity* (1944), or the possibly sexual bond between Ballen and Johnny Farrell in *Gilda* (1946). In all of these cases, the men have one another, and the "femme fatale," like the Mame in Gilda's song, takes the blame, becomes the debased object of investigation: the inevitable by-product of a system that has constructed the "femme fatale" as a projection of threats to the homosocial fabric of society.

The point is well exemplified in Sam Spade's bizarre speech at the end of *The Maltese Falcon* (1941). Although Spade has shown utter contempt for Miles Archer when Archer was alive, and although Spade is obviously in love with Brigid O'Shaughnessey, he shows a sort of intense aloofness in describing the code he must live by, that demands his turning Brigid in:

> When a man's partner is killed he's supposed to do something about it. It doesn't make any difference what you thought of him. He was your partner, and you're supposed to do something about it. And, it happens we're in the detective business . . . well, when one of your organization gets killed, it's bad business to let the killer get away with it. Bad all around. Bad for every detective, everywhere.

While there is clearly a rationale for holding Brigid accountable for the murder, the strange, almost autistic delivery of the speech suggests a dissociation of affect that comes across as problematic—as rigid, as cold, and as an indication of the threat of losing control that Spade faces throughout the narrative. Spade's discipline defines his masculinity, in stark contrast to "the fat man" (aptly named Gutman) and the gay man (the "exotic" Cairo). Here, however, such discipline plays as perverse, as Spade's further explanation for turning Brigid in strongly suggests:

> Maybe I do [love you]. Well, I'll have some rotten nights after I've sent you over, but that will pass. If all I've said doesn't mean anything to you, then forget it and we'll make it just this: I won't because all of me wants to, regardless of consequences, and because you counted on that with me, the same as you counted on that with all the others.

The ironic tone here—the allusion to "some rotten nights"—resets the power dynamic, ending the narrative with Spade's recovery of his invulnerable stance as the "man [who] must go who is not himself mean"—except, I'm suggesting, he's a little mean. Despite Brigid's guilt, Sam Spade is a psychological bruiser. He is, as Naremore says, "an unusually ruthless hero" (53). Spade sleeps with Archer's wife, showing almost as much contempt for her as he obviously held for her husband, Miles. And he sleeps with Brigid, as Jake Gittes does with Evelyn, only in the end to turn her over to her doom (although Jake is unwitting, and Spade is all-knowing). *Chinatown* is tragic and traumatic because Evelyn is an innocent victim; but *The Maltese Falcon* is disturbing, in pychosocial gender terms. As is the case with its protagonist, Spade, the film's "slickness" is belied by the brutality necessary to maintain his masculine code. Indeed, as Effie says to Sam, "You're too slick for your own good."

In contrast to the hard-boiled detective, for whom the homosocial bonds uphold masculine codes of honor, the toughened *femme moderne* is truly alone, as Mae Doyle is, in *Clash by Night* (1952). "Home," she says, "is where you come when you run out of places." Mae Doyle's expectations for domestic contentment are diminished to the point that what she finds most attractive in Jerry is that he's a man "who isn't mean and doesn't hate women."

Similarly, for Ethel Whitehead in *The Damned Don't Cry*, life is fundamentally about exigency: *The Damned Don't Cry* focuses in part on the limitations placed on Ethel's life ("Don't talk to me about self-respect. That's something you tell yourself you got when you got nothing else."). The film then portrays Ethel's aggressive response to these limitations ("All I can think of are the years I've wasted. . . .Well I want that time. I want it desperately. I'm going to drain everything out of those years there is to get."). The film shows Ethel taking on the role of "femme fatale," but such status, the story lays bare, is a direct result of her limitations based on gender and social roles and her hard-boiled response to those limitations—both of which are presented, for the most part, sympathetically. In conventional film representations of women, there is little complex awareness of a role for woman as strong *and* oppressed, even though this is surely a more apt description of modern women struggling for independence. Ethel, a *femme moderne* who aggressively struggles to define her own understanding of freedom and empowerment, may be seen as a "femme fatale." However, Ethel Whitehead's noir identity is obscured according to the classifications on offer in discussions of classic Hollywood films. *The Damned Don't Cry* calls forth the label "woman's picture," which defines female space but not in a way that fosters new imaginings of female power. Indeed, the labeling serves to cordon off female craving for independence as something "other" than the more meaningful tough work of noir, which has tended strongly to take for granted the integrity of only the male protagonist's selfhood.

In *The Damned Don't Cry*, the men read Ethel as a "femme fatale," as Dave Bannion does Lucy Chapman in *The Big Heat.* Racketeer George Castleman says to Ethel (who also role-plays, as the utterly invented wealthy socialite Lorna Hansen Forbes), "You're so used to lying and cheating and double-crossing, you can almost make it seem good." While George is the one who induced Lorna to seduce Nick Prenta, George physically attacks her when she does so: "Pass out keys to all your friends," he says bitterly. Meanwhile, Nick, whom in the end Lorna is trying to protect, calls Lorna a "dirty tramp." When, at the end of the film, the reporters go to Ethel's home to cover the story of Prenta's and Castleman's deaths and the mystery surrounding "Lorna Hansen Forbes," they wonder about Ethel Whitehead's future: "Well, it must be pretty tough living in a place like this." "Tougher to get out. Think she'll try again?" "Wouldn't you?" With this feminist gesture, the narrative provocatively ends with a strongly sympathetic tone toward Ethel's plight and status as a hard-boiled female protagonist.

Another hard-boiled female protagonist appears in Sam Fuller's bizarre *The Naked Kiss*, released in 1964. In this film, Kelly (played by Constance Towers) transforms from outcast prostitute to town heroine. After the town turns on her and then restores her image when she is vindicated for her murder of the town philanthropist hero (when it is proved that he was in fact a psychotic pederast), Kelly says at the end of the film, "They sure put up statues overnight around here, don't they."

This is the cultural landscape that film noir, in its most subversive gestures, questions. The narrative of film noir, carefully attended to, incites a consideration of the interplay between real human experience and gender expectations that are wedded to a logic of binary opposition.

Movies like the ones I've discussed in this chapter take noir viewers to task for their approach to the "femme fatale." In 1974, *Chinatown* revealed the tragic implications of looking for a virtual rendering of one big containable idea of woman, as Jake Gittes, slick as he is, has no means for sympathetically imagining, thus processing, the complex victimization of Evelyn Mulwray. The seemingly mutually exclusive categories evoked by "she's my sister, she's my daughter" give way to the film's plea to develop a more compassionate set of responses to the complex brutality of real human experience. *Chinatown* reveals the tragic implications of reading women as one thing or its opposite. However, this is the challenge of the paradigm of the "femme fatale": ideation surrounding Evelyn Mulwray, for example, must confront the real complex experience of Evelyn Mulwray, and there must be a critical viewer present to identify the confrontation and draw insights from its presence. Such an exchange between the active viewer and critic, sensitive to the network of expectations surrounding the "femme fatale" and the nuanced presentation of her experience in most film noir movies, will certainly constitute a more productive model for reading film noir.

Finally, Fritz Lang's *The Blue Gardenia* presents a clear case of the productive value of deconstructing the "femme fatale" as a category. As E. Ann Kaplan says, "While the male discourse tried to define Norah as a *femme fatale*, we see rather that she is a victim of male strategies to ensnare her for something she did not do" (87). Such insights are the fruits of questioning the "femmes fatale" as a given. Following in the steps of Kaplan and Cowie, as both question the notion that noir is primarily a "male preserve" (Cowie, 125), I want to shift emphases from assuming a shared understanding of "femmes fatales" to engaging critical insight into the logic of the narrative and character development of particular texts. At that point, we can broaden our understanding of how social roles and gender fantasies (of men and women) intersect with and within film noir.

Film noir strongly indicates the problems that remain in our cultural imaginings of and about women. For all the feminist critique that has re-viewed attitudes toward gender and sexuality and for all the feminist attention that has been paid to the "femme fatale" as projection of male fears and desires, we remain as a culture confused about and ambivalent toward the status of women and whether or not the arrangement of cultural experience in terms of gender is empowering or merely essentializing, thus limiting our imagination of the roles that women can play in the world. I believe that the ongoing construction of gendered spaces in culture hasn't been resolved and that the continuities between pre-feminist, modern, and contemporary culture haven't been adequately explored. Film noir offers a window through which we see this continuity. However, we need to reframe the "femme fatale" not as a given but as a critical apparatus for helping us to understand the limits of social roles and cultural fantasies about women.

In her collection of essays *Women in Film Noir*, E. Ann Kaplan argues that *The Blue Gardenia* is different from other film noirs, "reversing the situation in most noir films, where women are seen only within the male discourse [whereas] here that discourse is demystified through the fact that Norah is allowed to present herself directly to us" (85). In some sense defining the women in exceptional noir films who aren't really "femmes fatales" begs the issue, since the comparison depends on an a priori "femme fatale" which is drawn from the many films that, read closely, reveal the absence of a "femme fatale": she exists as an effect of problems in the culture, not as a thing in herself. Kaplan says that *The Blue Gardenia* presents "the confusion and alienation of women in a male world" (81). I suggest that this logic pertains far more widely in film noir, permeating the representation of so-called femmes fatales, than we are able to discern because of our preoccupation with categories of representation that are fixed and independent of experience rather than evolving critical tools.

2

"Well, aren't we ambitious": Desire, Domesticity, and the "Femme Fatale," or "You've made up your mind I'm guilty": The Long Reach of Misreadings of Woman as Wicked in American Film Noir

In this chapter, I want to focus more sharply on the misreadings of women, first by the men whom they encounter within the films, and second, by film viewers and critics who then perpetuate, and eventually institutionalize, these misreadings. The first part of my title comes from an early scene in *The Postman Always Rings Twice*, the film adapted from James Cain's novel and directed by Tay Garnett in 1946. *Postman*, featuring John Garfield as Frank Chambers and Lana Tuner as Cora Smith, remains a central text in the original-cycle of film noir movies made in the postwar period. In the scene from which my title is drawn, Frank sarcastically responds to Cora's declaration about the Twin Oaks, the roadside diner where she lives and works with her drunken but seemingly innocuous husband Nick. Unsatisfied, Cora has ambition: "I want to make something of this place. I want to make it into an honest to goodness—." Frank, a drifter who comes to the diner answering a "Man Wanted" sign, interrupts Cora's speech, "Well, aren't we ambitious." At that point Frank claims her expression of desire as his own, and kisses her, as the music swells.

Frank's dismissal of Cora's ambition represents a common rejection by characters in film noir of women's subjectivity, their desires and dreams for richer (fuller and more productive) lives. Instead, film noir's male protagonists project their own desires and fears onto women, which often results in casting psychologically three-dimensional, albeit hard-boiled, female characters as "femmes fatales." This process explains the second part of my title, quoted earlier in Chapter 1 and taken from the scene in Otto Preminger's *Laura*, in which Laura accuses Mark McPherson of just the kind of projection that is, I believe, in play when we talk about representations of women in noir (Figure 2.1).

Figure 2.1   "You've made up your mind I'm guilty." *Laura* (Gene Tierney) and McPherson (Dana Andrews) in *Laura* © 1944 Twentieth Century Fox. All rights reserved. (George Eastman House).

Laura's expression in the figure reflects a cynicism caused by McPherson's interrogation and distrust of her. The still captures an important moment in male–female relationships in film noir, one of the crucial narrative points at which men demonstrate suspicious ideation about women (sublimated in McPherson's case into his obsessive-compulsive play with a hand-held baseball game). Further, one of my central points in this chapter is that, as viewers, we often ally ourselves with male protagonists such as McPherson, violating the spirit of the representation of female characters in these films by superimposing the strict terms of the "femme fatale" onto them.

Our own viewing habits of reading women in film noir are, in other words, overly influenced by flawed male protagonists such as McPherson, or another suspicious protagonist like Devlin (Cary Grant) in *Notorious* (1946), who attributes a generalized badness to Alicia as opposed to extending sympathy to her complex experience and history (Figure 2.2). Further, Devlin subjects Alicia Huberman (Ingrid Bergman) to a "love test," as she calls it, just as McPherson does to Laura in the interrogation scene.

Figure 2.2 Devlin (Cary Grant) and Alicia Huberman (Ingrid Bergman) in *Notorious* (1946). Hulton Archive/Getty Images.

Alicia's hard-boiled demeanor and her cynicism are in large part caused by Devlin's mean distrust of her. She implores him to say that she doesn't need to take the government job that will require her to seduce Alex Sebastian: "Oh, darling, what you didn't tell them, tell me, that you believe I'm nice, that I love you, that I'll never change back." Dev's cold reply, "I'm waiting for your answer," constitutes his "love test," which, as he later confirms in the racetrack scene, she has failed. It is no wonder, then, that Alicia takes on the role of hard-boiled female, given "not a word of faith" she receives from Devlin: "What a little pal you are," she says to him: "never believing in me . . . just down the drain with Alicia—oh, Dev; oh, Dev."

Alicia's cynicism is propelled by Devlin's own aloofness and mistrust of her. Later in the film, as she cries during their exchange about her having "chalked up another boyfriend" with Sebastian, Dev brands her as the "femme fatale," confirming that he must have been crazy to think "that a woman like you could ever change her spots" and disregarding the trap laid for Alicia, who will be deemed a traitor or a whore by Dev and his colleagues. As in so many film noir movies, *Notorious* provides a narrative context for understanding why the so-called bad woman makes the difficult choices she makes—and yet, Dev's cruelty toward Alicia's overtures ("right below the belt every time," she says during one of their exchanges) demonstrates obsessive ideation about women that shapes our viewing alliances. Further, the misreading of women by men within these films extends into popular and scholarly writing on film noir, making it even more difficult to wrest the women in noir from the often-damaging discourse surrounding the "femme fatale."

Gilda, for example, "[evokes] for many the epitome of the noir's 'femme fatale,'" (Silver and Ursini, *Noir Style*, 96), and yet most viewers recognize that the film itself (rather than the icon of Gilda as it has evolved in popular culture) presents Gilda as sympathetic and victimized by the men around her. Gilda, says Andrew Britton, "is a film *about* misogyny" (220).[1] My claim is that in most film noir movies, sympathy is afforded to the female characters too simply categorized as "femmes fatales" by critics and popular discourse. Apart from the canonical baddies who are opaque, such as Phyllis Dietrichson and Brigid O'Shaughnessy, most noir females are presented in a context that helps us to understand why they behave the way they do. Thus Nicole Rafter's reference to the "sly money-hungry seductress who inhabits most film noirs" (25) misleads readers as to the tone and complexity of the representation of women in noir. My aim here is to shift discussion of women in noir away from a unilateral understanding of the "femme fatale," as understood in a positive or negative light by feminist critics (and as understood in a troubling way by popular discourse and some film criticism that objectifies women in noir as simply "bad") to more sustained attention paid to the psychosocial representation of female narrative in noir. The recentering of film noir criticism on women's stories, as Cowie, Hanson, and some of the essays in the second edition of *Women in Film Noir* do, will encourage a richer understanding of these films' treatment of gender and readings of film noir that are more in keeping with the subversive spirit of film noir generally.

Most accounts of the "femme fatale," for example, focus on her dangerous sexuality as an identifying feature and weapon. Certainly in many film noir movies, the hard-boiled woman's sexuality identifies the woman's role as a threat to gender conventions. However, these female characters are more often distinguished by desires defined more broadly: for example, they evince ambition to transgress or transcend conventional female gender roles, and/or the desire to exact richer lives (in terms of experience generally) than poverty or modern middle-class existence affords women. Most characters commonly identified as "femmes fatales" are sexual, but it's their unconventionality rather than their sexuality that makes them compelling. There's nothing unconventional about the "bad" woman (say, in Mrs. Duncan in *The Big Heat*, since she's simply bad), but Joan Crawford's and Barbara Stanwyck's noir roles, largely about ambition for fulfillment, combine elements of sexuality, the maternal, a desire for freedom from convention, and a vivacity that complicate a reductive reading of these characters as either "femmes fatales" or "good girls." Critical writing about the "femme fatale" often resists acknowledgment of the complexity and psychological depth of women in noir.

Consider, for example, Foster Hirsch's *Detours and Lost Highways* (1999), which offers a great many insights into noir and neo-noir. Hirsch is also the author of the excellent book *The Dark Side of the Screen: Film Noir* (1981, 2001). Hirsch's treatment of the "femme fatale" figure in his more recent book, however, repeats a pattern of reading women according to an overly narrow conception of the "femme fatale" figure. Hirsch has the following to say about Cora Smith in *The Postman Always Rings Twice*:

> One look and Frank's a goner. Turner was an exemplary Hollywood-made mannequin who walked like a beauty contestant and spoke in a studio-trained voice that had been scrubbed free of any signs of individual identity. As a performer, she simply put herself on display; she's an obedient young woman who emotes in a purely manufactured style. Her performance as Cora has no depth or resonance, and wasn't meant to. Following the mold created by James Cain, her character is simply a cheap, sexy blonde who sets a "real man" on fire.
>
> (56)

Hirsch makes a good point in contrasting the earthy Cora Papadakis in the novel with the more glamorous representation of Cora Smith by Lana Turner in the film. However, the contrast shouldn't keep us from reading the film on its own terms and in relation to other representations of women, domesticity, and desire in film noir. While it is the case that the novel is preoccupied with presenting Cora in animal terms (language about biting hell cats and cougars is almost obsessively repeated in the first pages of the novel), in the film, Cora's ambition to "be somebody" and make a successful business of the Twin Oaks (beyond her place as wife and cook) characterizes her subjectivity. She is hailed by critics as one of the central film noir "femmes fatales," American Movie Channel's website deeming Turner's Cora "one of the hottest portrayals of a sultry and seductive *femme fatale*" (Dirks). The film's presentation of her is, however, more complicated than is traditionally allowed by the label. With Phyllis Dietrichson, Cora has been dubbed "two of the [femme fatale's] most powerful screen incarnations" (Spicer, 91), and yet Cora is shown by the film to be desperately confined and victimized by the limitations imposed on her desires and her ambition by the enforcement of conventional domesticity. This point is best exemplified by a scene I alluded to in Chapter 1 in which Nick tells Cora, as is seen in the image below, that instead of working to build the Twin Oaks into a successful business, the Smiths will be moving to Northern Canada to take care of Nick's half-paralyzed sister.

Northern Canada figures here as a withdrawal from a place of possibility for Cora, as well as a cold cancellation of her desire; the paralysis of Nick's sister represents the helplessness of Cora to act on her desires. The image of paralysis is forcefully carried over in the shot that ends this scene, as Cora walks up the stairs into the darkness, arms paralyzed by her side, stunned and defeated. That in this scene the otherwise ineffectual Nick claims the privileges of patriarchy—he demands that Cora become domestic nursemaid to his sister ("what was good enough for my father is good enough for me")—foregrounds the patriarchal traditions Cora is up against. Also interesting is the fact that, in *The Noir Style*,

Figure 2.3 Northern Canada? Cora (Lana Turner), John Garfield (Frank Chambers), and Nick Smith (Cecil Kellaway) in *The Postman Always Rings Twice* (1946). Margaret Herrick Library. *The Postman Always Rings Twice* © Turner Entertainment Co. A Warner Bros. Entertainment Company. All Rights Reserved.

Silver and Ursini observe that Cora "completely dominates the frame" (121) as in Figure 2.3. Here, Cora is indeed standing between the sitting men; however, the scene reveals Cora to be caught between the two men and excluded from meaningful interaction. The conversation is between the two men; Nick disregards Cora while he explains the case to Frank. While one reading has Cora dominating the field of vision, a counter reading reveals that she is caught and excluded from the meaningful exchange between the male characters. The counter reading is made possible by focusing not upon Cora's sexuality, but by considering both her ambitions and fears. This makes her appear less of a "quintessential" "femme fatale," but rather a woman trapped by patriarchy and desperate about her situation.

Admittedly, Foster Hirsch defines Turner's Cora with rigidity in part to contrast Turner's portrayal with Jessica Lange's "tremulous" performance in the 1981 remake, but even in the comparison, Hirsch prescribes the original-cycle "femme fatale" in a way that suggests, to me quite strangely, a desire or need to maintain the category of the destructive "femme fatale" as fixed:

> Lange's sensitive, tremulous performance only reinforces the immutable noir logic that a "femme fatale" cannot be humanized: see Barbara Stanwyck in *Double Indemnity*.
>
> (60)

The "immutability" of noir logic is dependent upon a false assertion of the fixedness of the "femme fatale." Indeed, I want to contest the claim that there is an "immutable noir logic," since our experience of these films, and certainly what attracts us to them, is precisely their subversiveness, the contradictions that characterize their narrative and character patterns. I also want to point out the extent to which very few "femmes fatales" really fit the strict "femme fatale" model of evil, opaque woman who "cannot be humanized," which explains why Phyllis Dietrichson becomes canonized as the prototype for the "femme fatale" (recall Spicer's comment I quoted earlier about Phyllis and Cora representing the quintessential "femme fatale"). In fact, as I am suggesting, most "femme fatale" figures are distinctly humanized within the films, sometimes through plot and setting, sometimes through our awareness of the villainy of the male protagonist, and sometimes through the star text or screen presence of the actress playing the lead female role.

One central obstacle to becoming more sensitive to the portrayals of female experience in film noir is the rigid way feminist perspectives are conceived of by some critics. Hirsch claims, referring to Cain's *Postman*, "The original material was not written under a feminist watch and can profit little from a humanizing feminist perspective." (56). Neither was Chaucer's *Canterbury Tales* written under a modern "feminist watch," and yet this has not delegitimized reading the Wife of Bath's tale as a text that has things to tell us about language, class, and female power. The defensive tone of phrases such as "feminist watch" keeps Hirsch, I think, from engaging the diversity of feminisms and their potential for helping us to understand the role of the "femme fatale": the extent to which texts can be usefully subjected to a variety of feminist approaches in ways that will illuminate the text, the cultures that produced and were influenced by the texts, and the reading practices that affect (in some cases quite profoundly) the reception of the text in criticism and popular culture.

The point is not to dismiss one critic's reading of the "femme fatale" (especially important since critics such as Foster Hirsch and James Maxfield, whom I'll refer to later, have made significant contributions to the study of noir), but to examine the network of psychological and social expectations that inform our readings of these films and that may impede our ability to read these texts well. I think here, for example, of Kathie Moffett, the "femme fatale" figure who places second to Phyllis Dietrichson in the competition over which "femme fatale" is more awful, a "who's-worse" game my film noir students sometimes play with vigor. Says James Maxfield in *The Fatal Woman* at the beginning of his interesting chapter on *Out of the Past*:

> It is perhaps only my personal tastes that lead me to conclude that Jane Greer is the most attractive female lead of all the noir films of the forties; but certainly the character she plays in this film, Kathie Moffett, is a more plausible deceiver of men than earlier fatal females such as Phyllis Dietrichson or Helen Grayle. While it is difficult to imagine any man with reasonable intelligence and a survival instinct being taken in by the hard, obviously experienced, dyed blondes, Phyllis and Helen, it is much easier to believe that an otherwise intelligent private detective like Jeff Markham would accept the word of a soft, young, natural brunette like Kathy.
>
> (54)

The oddity of this extremely personal and impressionistic response, which falls away from the surrounding text, exemplifies a habit of projecting ideation about the "femme fatale" onto real women. This kind of blurred association of women in noir with gender phantoms keyed to "real life" results in a continual reassertion of the "femme fatale" as a fixed object and category.

The effects of extreme gender ideation on readings of film noir can be seen, as well, in the psychological typing of fictional characters undertaken by Scott Snyder in his "Personality Disorder and the Film Noir Femme Fatale," published in the *Journal of Criminal Justice and Popular Culture* in 2001. Snyder extends fatal-woman affect to the women themselves who performed in film noir movies:

> The famed *film noir* actresses themselves often possessed a physiognomy and cinematic presence reflective of Cluster B personalities. Barbara Stanwyck, the "undisputed first lady of *noir*," had a scornful, taut face and voice. Her posture was tight and defensive in keeping with a tough screen presence. A deadly, cold, sensuality characterized many of her films. Veronica Lake's face barely moved. Her voice and bearing were notable for their angularity, frigidity, and sleekness. She was shy, yet sexy, with a hazy, muddled quality; chiseled features and flawless beauty highlighted by a translucent Nordic complexion completed the picture. An efficient, dominating, wise-cracking quality set her apart. Joan Crawford had a screen persona characterized by fierceness, willfulness, and an almost diabolical, tyrannical ferocity with which she fought her enemies. She could dispatch men without compunction.
>
> (162–3)

The quote demonstrates a collapse of distinctions among realms: the actress herself; the "femme fatale" persona; even publicity clichés, since the final sentence is strikingly similar to Warner Brothers' own advertising for film noir in the 1940s. Such blurring needs to be examined as one piece in the puzzle of how and why the "femme fatale" has been constructed and why the category has remained so central to readings of noir over the years. The category of the "femme fatale," projected across the realms of representation and the real, fulfills a need that seems quite persistent in the culture to scapegoat women whose lives don't follow an easily digestible pattern and whose choices invite far more negative criticism than the "High Plains Drifter" (or the detective who walks the mean streets, not himself mean) is subjected to for his moral limitations and ambiguities.

Another obstacle to becoming more sensitive to the complexity of women's stories in noir is the model of reading film narrative teleologically, viewing practices that privilege what happens at the end. Reading the conclusion as a final "message" concerning the film's meaning often misrepresents the tone and character of the film. Indeed, this kind of linear understanding of narrative seems out of keeping with the ruptures in gender representation in film noir. For example, some feminist critics provide evidence for these films being sexist by pointing toward the endings that suppress female characters without recognizing, first, that it's no surprise that in a sexist culture, film and literature would often reflect those gender biases; and second, that not only do noir films tend to resist and unleash anxiety and emotion attending to conventional role-playing, but they also often undermine the supposed controlling force of the narrative, usually male, by focusing on the women's stories within the narrative.

Thus a feminist essay such as Grant Tracey's in the fourth volume of the *Film Noir Reader*, "Covert Narrative Strategies to Contain and Punish Women in *The Big Heat* and *The Big Combo*," examines the victimization of the women in these films, an important element of film noir movies, but fails to observe the extent to which *the films make that victimization clear*. In other words, the women's stories in these films often cast severe doubt on the controlling male narrative, just as Karen Hollinger discusses in her important essay on this topic. Hollinger suggests that the strong female presence in voice-over film noirs such as *Laura*, *Gilda*, and *The Lady from Shanghai* confounds the controlling male narrative. This helps to explain how these films become available for feminist discussion. (An analogous observation might be Mary Ann Doane's and Richard Dyer's that Gilda's active first gesture of throwing her hair back, which fills the screen, challenges and resists the objectifying male gaze.) Hollinger in fact suggests that *The Lady from Shanghai* never makes it clear whether Elsa Bannister, a canonical "quintessential" "femme fatale," is a victimizer or victimized, whether she "partakes of [Bannister's] evil or has merely been victimized by it" (257). Andrew Britton also suggests that while "it is so terribly difficult to deduce what [Elsa] is really like from what she appears to be," there are grounds for a more nuanced reading of her in the context of the cynical tone of the film and her own seeming "helplessness and despair": "After confessing," continues Britton, "that she has contemplated suicide 'many times,' Elsa declares—in what seems to be good faith—her conviction that 'everything's bad' and that 'you can't escape it or fight it'" (218) (Figure 2.4).

Again, such an observation helps us to wonder constructively whether our emphasis on the "quintessential" "femme fatale" is largely

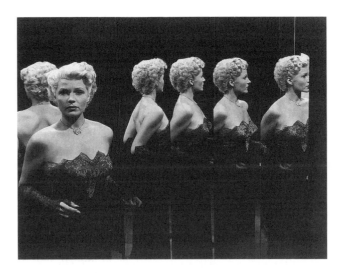

Figure 2.4   No escape: Elsa Bannister (Rita Hayworth) and the mirrors in *The Lady from Shanghai* (BFI), copyright 1948, renewed 1975 Columbia Pictures Industries, Inc. All rights reserved. Courtesy of Columbia Pictures.

a result of our habit, once again, of assuming a straightforwardness to the male narrative that finally doesn't obtain when we look closely at the films and at their investment in women's stories. "Whose story," Elizabeth Cowie asks, "does the film tell?" (137). Whose side, moreover, are the films on? *Gilda* is certainly not on Johnny Farrell's side, which again should lead us to question the common labeling of Gilda as "one of the all-time great classic 'femme fatales'" (Biesen, 169). Biesen herself acknowledges that "Gilda is not evil or malicious, but instead a victim of the misogynistic, violent men around her as she becomes involved in a series of bizarre, dysfunctional relationships that accentuate her gender distress" (170). Yet such an observation hasn't led us as viewers and critics to reimagine our ways of conceiving of the "femme fatale" as a dynamic tool of critique rather than a centrally "bad" object of investigation. Tracey's essay makes the good point that in *The Big Combo*, Susan becomes "a controlling subject, rendering guilty the very man who had put her in an abject position with regard to the law" (129). This reading captures the film's interest in Susan well and suggests that the film is available for feminist discussion in a way that the larger argument of Tracey's essay does not.

I also want to identify the problem of overvaluing role modeling that I referred to in my introduction, a persistent notion that the only valid feminist representations are ones that present heroic females, ă lă Norma Rae, who manage against the odds to transcend the boundaries placed on or around them. As a part of a feminist project to analyze film and media representation, this seems important. But when modeling becomes valorized as the only truly feminist kind of representation, we lose the opportunity to examine the stresses and tensions surrounding representations that really can help us to decipher the more difficult (as opposed to the more obvious) forms of gender bias and oppression. I think that Tracey's judgment of *The Big Heat* and the *The Big Combo*, for example, is based on an idea of modeling good men and women that isn't appropriate to an art form that remains compelling because of the complexity of its portrait of society and gender relations. Film noir movies do indeed push against the enforcement of gender boundaries by presenting women as varied and complex, and as responsive to social changes that empowered and also at times victimized them. Film noir films reflect anxieties that help us to see how limited cultural discourse about empowered and empowering women remains.

Andre de Toth's *Pitfall* (1948) is an excellent example of a film noir movie with wonderfully jumbled portraits of gender and a tone of moral ambiguity that calls into question our knee-jerk characterizations of noir men and women. We learn early in this film that Bill Smiley has been sent to jail for submitting false claims to an insurance company in order to buy a fur coat, diamond ring, and a motor boat for his girlfriend Mona Stevens, played by Lizabeth Scott. Dick Powell plays middle-class suburban John Forbes, the insurance man with a wife and son sent to reclaim from Mona the gifts Smiley had given to her. Forbes has an affair with Mona, which angers MacDonald, a detective working for the insurance company who wants Mona for himself; MacDonald, played with scary gusto by Raymond Burr, stalks Mona, then beats Forbes up to intimidate him. When Smiley gets out of jail, he finds out about Forbes and goes to his home, where Forbes ends up killing him. Forbes's is a self-defense case, so he is let go; however, when Mona kills the brutal MacDonald, she is sent to jail for murder at the end of the film.

While *Pitfall* has been read as a conservative allegory about the dangers of straying from middle-class suburban life, the film in fact portrays Lizabeth Scott's *femme moderne* character with sympathy, interest, and subtlety. The story charts John Forbes's mid-life crisis that presumably leads him into his adulterous affair with Mona Stevens. The film begins with our introduction to the stalwartly and monosyllabically named John Forbes, who lives in the suburbs with his wife Sue (played notably by Jane Wyatt, who would gain fame six years later as a domestic icon as the mother in television's *Father Knows Best*). The couple has a son, Tommy, who repeatedly lionizes his daddy as the hard-boiled hero in the family, wanting to hear stories about the war, disappointed to find out that his dad was stationed in Denver, Colorado rather than on a romantic and violent front line abroad. *Pitfall*'s first scene introduces Sue making eggs. "Breakfast is on the table," she says. "Where else would it be?" Forbes replies, demonstrating middle-class malaise and a mid-life crisis. Sue tries to cheer Forbes up by reminding him, "You're John Forbes, average American, backbone of the country." Forbes's reply, "I want somebody to be the backbone and hold me up," suggests the burdens of masculine role-playing, a deflation of gender roles reinforced when Mona Stevens first meets Forbes, who comes to her house to reclaim Smiley's gifts: "You're a little man with a briefcase," says Mona.

Mona's insight not only develops the film's theme of the burden of gender roles but establishes her as sympathetic and in many ways the moral center of the film. As Mona catalogs the things Smiley gave to her when she first meets Forbes, she says, "Why is it that people grow attached to things that don't really matter at all?" She explains to Forbes why she was with Smiley: "I liked Smiley mostly because he was nice to me," a comment that suggests that normal life for Mona, as is the case for so many female characters in film noir, doesn't include nice guys but bad men, brutes, and gangsters.

Certainly the film's representation of Mona's dark experience with all the men in the film justifies her low expectations. Forbes has an affair with her and doesn't tell her he's married; MacDonald stalks Mona, who says when she first meets Forbes that MacDonald "nearly scared me to death." Mona's desperation with regard to MacDonald eventually leads to her shooting him and becoming the film's scapegoat, which is underscored as the police detective lectures Forbes on his getting off scot-free after killing Smiley ("Just a little call to the police and you could have avoided all this mess. No, you kill a man, and that's not a pleasant thing to live with for the rest of your life. Or don't things like that bother you?"). Mona's marginalized role is prefigured earlier in the film, when she learns that Forbes is home sick one day (really home recovering from his beating from MacDonald). Mona drives to his house to deliver chicken soup. Realizing as she approaches the house that the woman standing outside of it is Forbes's wife, Mona says, "I think I'm on the wrong street," a comment that resonates with Mona's status as a permanent outsider.

And yet despite the sympathy that Mona elicits, she's also clearly defined as a hard-boiled female character, a *femme moderne* whose desires and ambition are articulated in her owning a profession (about modeling, she says, "that's my business"); in her desire to be with a nice guy; and in her love of adventure, sailing with her hair in her face, while beside her, John Forbes sits stiffly with his hat on doing double takes at Mona every time the boat changes gear or makes a turn. If the film is ambivalent about the domestic life John Forbes leads before he meets Mona and his criminal life later in the film, it seems remarkably unambiguous about its eliciting sympathy for Mona Stevens. Thus the film's promotional tag line is quite stunning: "A man can be as strong as steel . . . but somewhere there's a woman who'll break him!" The promotion deeply misrepresents the tone and character patterns in the film—"the unforgettably exciting story of one man's pitfall . . . a pitfall with lips too warm . . . and a heart too cold!" (*Pitfall* Press book, BFI). The film belies such a characterization of Mona, who is portrayed with warmth and sympathy, while *Pitfall*'s promotion materials perversely project the role of "femme fatale" onto her. As in so many film noir movies, the woman labeled as dissembler has a story of her own.

And yet, in the case of *Pitfall*, the promotional tag is a fascinating misprision, since the only way in which Mona could be conceived of as a "breaker" of men, a "femme fatale" of sorts, is in her power to elicit desire in others. Mona says of Smiley, "He was too much in love with me." This is a way of understanding smart, beautiful, and powerful women that recurs in both critical and popular ideations, one that is clear in critical approaches to advertising executive Laura Hunt, a figure discussed earlier. *Laura* is a film centrally concerned with male projection, desire, and working women, but the critical focus has been less on Laura's ambition and more on her alluring sexuality. Eugene McNamara says about Laura, her "beauty is dangerous to men, as is the beauty of all Fatal Women. But, unlike the classic Fatal Woman, Laura is unconscious of her power" (29). McNamara's analysis is strangely incoherent, since the essay is sympathetic toward the representation of Laura but can't keep from dismissing her. Without making explicit the connections between the myth of the fatal woman and our projections of mystery and villainy onto innocent women, the essay elicits such analysis. Male desire, as in Lydecker's and McPherson's obsessions in the film *Laura*, redounds destructively on women. McNamara ends his essay with an overdetermined example of just such denial of female subjectivity in favor of projection: "And Laura herself? In her distant niche, forever out of reach. Remember, she's only a dream" (29).

Cultural difficulty in responding to realistically complex and divided portraits of ambitious women leads us in many cases to impose or project restrictive categories on the *femmes modernes* portrayed in film noir. Readings of *Mildred Pierce*, for example, are a good illustration of such limited purview. Mildred Pierce struggles to advance her professional life as she spoils her selfish and status-obsessed daughter Veda. Many viewers, including feminist film critics, have seen the film as an attack on bad mothers. Nina Liebman, for example, argues that the film blames Mildred's ambition and concludes by reinstating patriarchy and casting husband Bert as the final figure of authority and worth. Liebman echoes Veda's own charge against Mildred—"It's your fault I'm the way I am"—but certainly we're not supposed to identify with Veda's point of view. The film portrays Mildred's plight sympathetically, from her desperate initial near-suicide (which looks forward to Crawford's aimless meandering the city streets at the beginning of her next noir film, *Possessed*) through her ambition to leave her unemployed and unfaithful husband, whose affair with "Mrs. Beiderhoff" seems intended to restore a masculinity Bert feels is lacking at home with his enterprising wife Mildred, who bakes pies to sell to neighbors for extra cash (Figure 2.5).

Figure 2.5 Mildred (Joan Crawford) baking pies, *Mildred Pierce* (1945) BFI; *Mildred Pierce* © Turner Entertainment Co. A Warner Bros. Entertainment Company. All Rights Reserved.

Indeed, Mildred's story provides a perfect example of Sylvia Harvey's claim that "[t]he family, within a capitalist economy, has functioned both objectively and subjectively as the locus of women's particular oppression" (*Women in Noir*, 1980, 33).

Mildred's spoiled treatment of Veda remains the critical crux in readings of this film, with judgments on Mildred's "bad parenting" the source for locating her as "the problem" in this story. I would suggest that a shift in orientation, from Mildred's character to a wider view (seeing, with Sylvia Harvey, the "disfigurement of the family" as film noir's subversiveness [33]), allows for greater understanding of the film's representation of family, work, gender roles, and postwar reflections on the American Dream. As I suggested earlier, this reorientation would also move us away from reading films backward from the ending, as if the often patched-up conventional "happy ending" were tantamount to the spirit of the film. (*Gilda'* s strangely ameliorative ending is a good example of such arbitrary tack-ons: Gilda's comment, "neither one of us has to apologize because we were both such stinkers," frustrates viewers who have witnessed Johnny be so much more of a stinker—as Dyer says, "it is Gilda/Hayworth who is known and normal, and Johnny who is unknown and deviant" ["Resistance," 121].) Certainly *Mildred Pierce* recovers Bert as a positive force toward the end of the film, but that change is only a result of Bert's growing respect for Mildred's independence and self-sufficiency. In the end, Mildred is endorsed by Bert, not patriarchically dominated by him, as she is at the beginning of the film.

Then, too, the film's representation of Mildred's mothering shouldn't, I think, be reduced to a commentary on "bad mothering," a reading suggested by one of the film's taglines, "A mother's love leads to murder" (given, in retrospect, added extratextual weight, once Crawford's "Mommy Dearest" persona began to be cultivated). Instead, I think Mildred's role as mother can best be understood as a kind of extreme overinvestment, in keeping with postwar anxieties about female ambition and desire. Mildred is working hard to be successful and powerful—in terms of making things happen—in the realms of family and business. Her excessive attention to Veda is a response to the pressures of role-playing, and her overinvestment in her mother role makes self-sabotage an inevitability. Such crumbling under the pressures of ambition and desire allies Mildred with a character like Walter Neff from *Double Indemnity*, who also embarks on a suicidal overinvestment. Mildred is smart and she's attractive—not necessarily sexual, although the promotional posters for the film, as in the misleading captions for

Pitfall, situate her as a dangerous "femme fatale" figure. Warner Brothers promoted Mildred Pierce as a bad woman—"She's the kind of woman men want . . . but shouldn't have!" (*Mildred Pierce*, Press book, BFI), misrepresenting the character. The perspective is interestingly bulwarked by popular commentary such as Eddie Muller's in his discussion of the film in *Dark City* (1998). With a tone equal to the original trailers and taglines (as in Snyder's analysis of the affect of noir actresses, as quoted earlier), Muller says of Mildred, "She'd dig her high heels into anyone's back to gain purchase in the social register" (60). Muller goes so far as to label Mildred an ultimate "femme fatale," a "hydra-headed woman—mother, moneymaker, homemaker, whore" (60), which should surprise anyone familiar with the film's portrait of this ambitious, hard-working, and concerned female character.

Muller's description of Mildred, "in her rise from hash-slinger to cutthroat capitalist," elides the whole of the story. In *Mildred Pierce*, Mildred is betrayed not only by Veda but also by her husband Monte and her partner Wally, who sell her interests in the business she built out from under her. Muller explicitly cultivates the blurring of Mildred's character with Joan Crawford's life, a breakdown of a distinction of realms discussed earlier ("Like Mildred," Muller says, "[Crawford] was ruthless in her quest for the brass ring. . . . If this sounds suspiciously like the plot of a film noir, wait—it gets thicker" [60]). Muller's investment in describing Mildred as having "left a succession of husbands and lovers emasculated" (60) is again tonally off-point, but also strangely echoes general anxieties concerning women competing for power and the "femme fatale's" busting up of manhood (Muller later refers to Crawford's own "ball-breaking bluntness").[2] Such projections are, I argue throughout this project, a repetition of patterns of misreading women presented within the films themselves. Further, promotion, advertising, and film criticism collude in some cases to recast a film's sympathetic representation of female struggle and agency as malevolent, as in the "special teaser" promotion Warner Brothers employed to excite interest in the film: "Please don't tell anyone what Mildred Pierce did" (*Mildred Pierce* Press book, BFI). In fact, the film sympathetically examines the difficulties of balancing postwar realities of female drive and ambition with traditional gender roles.

Crime of Passion (1957), made more than a decade later, also addresses such difficulties for women of balancing gender expectations and the realities of female desire and ambition. Barbara Stanwyck plays Kathy Ferguson, a successful San Francisco newspaper reporter. The film portrays intense gender anxieties, as Kathy falls for police officer Bill Doyle (played by the underrated actor Sterling Hayden), moves to the suburbs, and becomes obsessed with competing with other suburban wives trying to push their husbands up the social and professional ladder. The portrayal of life in the suburbs is a striking register of extreme gender anxiety and social illness, as Kathy reacts with increasing hysteria to her environment. The naturalist curve of the story is prefigured when Kathy explains to Bill on their first date that marriage isn't for her: "For marriage, I read life sentence. For home life, I read TV nights, beer in the fridge, second mortgage. Unh unh, not for me. For me, life has to be more than that." Kathy's ambition stands in contrast to the conventional male view espoused by the film's antagonist, Officer Alito, Bill's partner, who says to Kathy (as she breaks a murder case by nabbing a murderess through an open column she writes to "all the women out there"), "Your work should be raising a family, having dinner ready when your husband comes home."

When Kathy first arrives at her house in the suburbs, Bill asks, "What do you think of the neighborhood," and she answers, with palpable unease, "Right now, I'm not thinking about the neighborhood." The film's attack on gender roles and their stranglehold on female independence appears in two scenes in which Kathy listens to a gathering of her husbands' colleagues' wives, at first, talking about their husbands' ambitions for promotion, and then, preoccupied with the "cream cheese and olives." Trapped, she escapes to the kitchen where the men play poker and discuss finances, a conversation, with verbal hysteria, she tries to participate in, to the embarrassment of her husband Bill. Kathy's alienation in the world of suburban wives is a measure of how out of place she is in conventional gender spaces, and the film deals with her oppression overtly. When Bill calls her "Angel," she says, "Please don't call me Angel. I loathe it." The comment is reminiscent of Virginia Woolf's speech to the Women's Service League, in which she famously disparaged the Victorian "angel in the house": "I turned upon her and caught her by the throat. I did my best to kill her. My excuse, if I were to be had up in a court of law, would be that I acted in self-defence. Had I not killed her she would have killed me" ("Professions for Women," 1931; 1988). Woolf's comments—her insistence that killing the phantom of the angel was crucial to her own survival—predict Kathy's tragic end, as Kathy fails in her struggle to escape the gender phantoms that haunt her.

Crime of Passion takes an interesting turn when it shifts its object of criticism from gender roles to more generalized middle-class existence, as Kathy's drive to help her passive husband rise up through the ranks of the department eventually lands her in bed with his superior, Inspector Pope (Raymond Burr). Kathy has sex with him in order to ensure that her husband is promoted to the Inspector's job when he retires. Such desperate gestures demonstrate Kathy's sublimation of her own ambition into an extreme need to see her husband succeed—thus the gender anxiety is transposed into an analysis of middle-class complacence, which would be more palatable to 1957 audiences than a full-blown critique of gender. Kathy's impulse to sleep with Inspector Pope (and, indeed, the scene is presented as a result of impulse, rather than a planned rendezvous) backfires, when the Inspector turns on her, himself reading her as a "femme fatale" and going back on his word to promote Bill. In anger and a desperate need to justify her action, Kathy shoots and kills Pope, and her husband, ironically presented throughout the film as a mediocre police officer, cracks the case, discovers his wife's crime, and, as Sam Spade sacrifices Brigid O'Shaughnessey to restore masculine patriarchy, turns her in. The conventional system of law is validated, but the spirit of the story has been its critique of gender roles, conventional gendered spaces, and the oppression of women within these realms. Eddie Muller agrees that *Crime of Passion* is a "none-too-subtle condemnation of women's subordination, trapped in a curt conventional murder drama," although he attributes to the Jo Eisenger script the presentation of Kathy as a "sociopathic harpy" (67). Substituting an extreme stereotype for a character, Muller invokes language that reflects a unifaceted view of the strong determined female noir characters that is not only conflated with the category of "femme fatale" but also leads viewers away from an adequately complex view of the gender tensions that make these films so interesting.

In his DVD commentary on *Clash by Night* (1952), Stanwyck's next hard-boiled noir film (directed by Fritz Lang), Peter Bogdanovich says that the film is more a "triangle or love story" than a film noir movie. The comment reflects the same kind of strange exclusivity in conceiving of noir that characterizes much writing on film noir. The triangle is certainly a common noir trope, from *Double Indemnity* to *Gilda*, *Out of the Past*, and *Scarlet Street*. Then, too, if *Clash by Night* is a love story, it's certainly a perverse one, in which the male lover, Earl Pfeiffer (Robert Ryan), is a misogynist brute whom viewers can little identify with. Instead, the film, based on a Clifford Odets play, is a treatment of failed ambition, like so many noir films. The film is about disappointed American dreams and the violent distresses that lurk beneath middle-class life, especially for women in postwar America (Figure 2.6). Indeed, Lang himself commented that social changes regarding gender and marriage were

Figure 2.6　Mae Doyle (Barbara Stanwyck) and Earl (Robert Ryan) in *Clash by Night* © Turner Entertainment Co. A Warner Bros. Entertainment Company. All Rights Reserved. BFI.

an informing context for the film. Lang had read about "the background of the moral changes after the war, women working, not satisfied with just being housewives. I had also read an article about the increasing number of wives that would have affairs" (*Film Noir Reader 3*, 58).

In *Clash by Night*, Mae Doyle is a pessimistic drifter who refers to herself twice in the film as "hard-boiled." The possibilities on offer for Mae are represented by what we know of her past and in the portrait of Cannery-row fish-packer Peg, played by Marilyn Monroe. Of Mae's past, we know that she loved a politician "who didn't tear a woman down" and made her feel "more than herself, not less." When he died, he left her money but his family took her to court, and "I near drowned in his family's outrage." The social cards stacked against her, Mae contends with husband Jerry (Paul Douglas), whose brutally misogynist uncle thinks that "we spoil women in this country" and that women, like horses, should be whipped. Earl, the often drunk film projectionist, objectifies women in a way that literalizes Laura Mulvey's concerns about film and the male gaze when he makes a parallel between cutting up film images and cutting women: "Didn't you ever want to cut up a beautiful dame?" Such sadism runs through Earl's dialogue, like his comments about his itinerant wife: "Some day I'm going to stick her full of pins to see if blood runs out."

The high-angle shots of Mae talking about getting old and lonely, as she first resists marrying nice-guy Jerry, underscore her alienation as a woman with desires who understands the limits of middle-class gender roles: "Find yourself someone with a baby carriage," she says to Jerry, imploring him not to be "so eager to make a mistake" with her. "He thinks I'm Red Riding Hood," she later says of Jerry, a complaint that echoes other noir female insistence that the men see only what they want to see when they fall for women. Unlike Jerry, Earl recognizes Mae's sexuality, a point made through the camera's register of Mae's gaze on Earl, when he first appears in the film.

Jerry's ideation surrounding Mae shifts as so many male protagonists' visions of women do.[3] "You're rotten," says Jerry. "I know, Jerry," replies Mae. But the film doesn't present Mae as "rotten." The film presents Mae as lost in a modern and alien landscape where women should "expect nothing," as she says, and just get a little "older, duller, and a little stupider" as they age. Peg stands up for Mae, telling Mae's brother Joe, "You don't have the right to judge her," as she pushes at the edges of conventional womanhood, rebelling against Joe's simple calls for her to be passive: "What I'd really like," says Peg at the beginning of the film, "is a trailer, [to] cover the whole country seeing places." When Joe asks about the kids, she says, "Who said I'd have kids," to which he responds, simply, "You'd have kids." Peg complains to Mae, "I hate people bossing me. You marry a fella and the first thing he does is boss you." In the end, Peg falls into Joe's arms and Mae opts for "duties, obligations, responsibilities," but not before the film presents the roles that are governed by these values to be depressingly restrictive.

In Fritz Lang's next noir film, *Human Desire* (1954), Vicki Buckley, like Cora Smith in *Postman*, enjoins her lover to kill her husband as a result of feeling trapped within an oppressive domestic realm with a drunken husband Carl, played by Broderick Crawford. In both films, women's desire to "be somebody," to engage in life, to "work hard and be something," in Cora's words, is expressed, as is the prospect of killing their husbands, in terms of wanting something to happen. In *Gun Crazy*, Annie Laurie also characterizes her desires in terms of action: "I want action." In *Human Desire*, Vicki says, "Nothing ever happens to me" and then about Carl, "If only something would happen to him." Vicki echoes her yearning for a better life when she explains to Jeff why she married Carl: "I wanted a home. I wanted to belong. It isn't easy for a girl drifting around." In *Postman*, Cora explains to Frank why she married Nick, saying that she was tired of fighting "all the guys" off ("I never met a man since I was fourteen that didn't want to give me an argument about it," "it" being the way Cora looks). While Vicki (like Mona Stevens in *Pitfall*) is the victim of predatory men, she (Vicki) offers a striking comment on female experience: "Most women are unhappy; they just pretend they aren't." Glenn Ford's Jeff offers an omniscient male smiling reply to Vicki's feminist insight, "No they're not," which implicates him, as does the persuasiveness of Vicki's later criticism of Jeff when he takes the high road ("Your conscience didn't stop you from making love to me").

My point here is that Jeff is, within the logic of the narrative, a kind of homme fatale—admittedly not the same as, but subtly in tune with, the psychotic jealous men in noir: Bogart as Dix Steele (in Nicholas Ray's *In a Lonely Place* [1950] (Figure 2.7), Robert Ryan as Smith Ohlrig from Max Ophuls's *Caught* (1949) or Howard Wilton the gardener in *Beware My Lovely* (1952), Lawrence Tierney as Sam Wilde in Robert Wise's *Born to Kill* (1947), Ronald Colman as Anthony John in Cukor's *A Double Life* (1947), or Robert Walker as Bruno Anthony in Hitchcock's *Strangers on a Train* (1951).

How much less culpable are noir movies' nice guys, the men who are ostensibly seduced by "femmes fatales" but who are often responsible for the trauma and destruction that happens in these films as a direct result of their misreading of, or suspiciousness regarding, the women we label "femmes fatales"?

Figure 2.7   Laurel Gray (Gloria Grahame) and Dix Steele (Humphrey Bogart) in *In A Lonely Place* (1950). Columbia TriStar/Hulton Archive/Getty Images.

What would it mean to extend the role of the homme fatale in film noir to Humphrey Bogart's noir roles, such as Rip Murdoch in *Dead Reckoning*; the role he turned down in *Gilda*, Johnny Farrell, played by Glenn Ford; Glenn Ford's other male protagonist roles in Fritz Lang's films, Dave Bannion in *The Big Heat* and Jeff in *Human Desire*; Devlin in *Notorious*; even John Forbes, the seemingly harmless middle-class insurance man in *Pitfall*; or Jake Gittes, the character everyone misreads as a beleaguered noir protagonist who is profoundly implicated in *Chinatown*'s trauma. What about Guy Haines, Bruno's doppelganger in *Strangers on a Train*, who is largely responsible for his wife Miriam's murder? I ask the question because I don't believe that a full understanding of the forces of gender representation in noir can be gained without close examination of our skewed readings of women in these films and the gender psychosis of noir men (Frank Krutnik has done excellent work in this area in his *In a Lonely Street*). This last point is not one about clarity for the sake of understanding the postwar male experience (pace Krutnik), but about illuminating the forces working against women's interest in film noir and in western culture generally.

Paying close attention to the desperate and violent exploitation of women by men in noir also helps to reveal the inextricable link between the variety of crimes of the male protagonist and the construction of the "femme fatale" as an immutable category, a fixed given that predetermines our thinking about women in noir. As Angela Martin says in a comment that ends the second edition of Kaplan's *Women in Film Noir*:

> It is also clear that in most of these films women have ended up with bad partners and/or are victims of male violence, perversity or authority. But that in itself throws a different perspective on badness, which is, clearly, usually male in these films, not female.
>
> (222)

In *Dead Reckoning*, Rip Murdoch tries to discover what has happened to his war buddy Johnny, whom Rip says, "I knew . . . like my own birthmark." "After what we'd been through," says Rip, "we could read each other's minds." Contrasted with this representation certainly of homosocial and possibly homosexual intimacy, Rip considers the woman (Coral) he knows Johnny loves: "I wanted to see her the way Johnny had . . . maybe she was alright. And maybe Christmas comes in July." Such a priori suspiciousness, clearly linked to Rip's devotion to Johnny, suggests the inevitability of Coral's branding as "femme fatale," despite the film's sympathetic portrayal of her for most of the movie and the sympathetic portrayal of her death at the end of the film, Rip entreating her to "parachute" gently into the night.

Coral's role must be considered at least in part in relation to Rip's distrust of her and projection onto her throughout, a point about women taking on a tabula rasa role, illustrated in the fact that Lizabeth Scott has three names in the film, her "real" name, then the names by which Johnny and Rip call her (first Dusty, then Mike—names that not coincidentally increasingly deny her femininity, which poses such a threat in the film) (Figure 2.8). The larger notion of woman as threat appears with a Bogie flourish as Rip and Coral become acquainted. Rips says:

> Women ought to come capsule size, about four inches high. When a man goes out of an evening, he just puts her in his pocket and takes her along with him and that way, he knows exactly where she is. He gets to his favorite restaurant, he puts her on the table and lets her run around among the coffee cups while he swaps a few lies with his buddies. Comes time in the evening he wants her full size and beautiful. He waves his hand and there she is full size. But if she starts to interrupt he just shrinks her back to pocket size and puts her away.

Figure 2.8 Coral/Dusty/Mike (Lizabeth Scott) and Rip Murdoch (Humphrey Bogart) in *Dead Reckoning* (1947). George Lacks/Time & Life Pictures/Getty Images.

While Coral/Dusty/Mike initially responds that the speech is the "most conceited statement I've ever heard," she later glosses the comment in a way that suggests its centrality to the operation of the homme fatale: "Because you couldn't put her in your pocket you get all mixed up." Later, Rip says to her, "Get back in my pocket." Rip's overdetermined speech about controlling female power and action has an interesting extratextual reference point, since Lauren Bacall (whom Lizabeth Scott strongly resembles in *Dead Reckoning*) reports in her autobiography *Lauren Bacall by Myself* that

> Bogie had a joke dream—that a woman should be able to fit into a man's pocket. He'd take her out, talk to her, let her stand on the palm of his hand, dance on a table; when she got out of order—back in the pocket. And she could be made life-size when desired. And despite how wonderful he was, there were times when I would have liked to do the same thing to him.
>
> (176)

The ideation (Rip's, Bogart's) about containing female power provides another example of slippage between representation and the real. Rip's/ Bogart's domestic fantasy suggests not only the important exploration in film noir of a large-scale cultural preoccupation with female desire and ambition, but also an occasion for rebellion (of the sort I'm suggesting characterizes the stories of women in noir) against such containment, as in Bacall's response: "there were times when I would have liked to do the same thing to him."

In one sense, film noir movies demonstrate the violent consequences, not necessarily of changes in the social order, but of not recognizing the variety of perspectives on offer in stories of modern life, including the crucial point of view of the female subject. Closer attention to narrative logic in noir—the portraits of female ambition and the narrative impact of male suspiciousness of women, both narrative operations, I've been arguing, obscured by an overreliance on the "femme fatale" figure—can play a crucial role in broadening our methods for reading these films. Such a shift in orientation may not only help to unearth the female stories and gender trauma represented in film noir—distressing narratives that surely at times characterize modern and contemporary social interaction—but may also contribute to a more sustained fascination with the films themselves, rather than the gendered clichés of aggressive female sexuality that hover around our reading and discussions of film noir. A more vigorous cultivation of discussions about female ambition and insight might transform the "femme fatale"—in popular *and* academic discourse—into something more complicated and meaningful than a figure of fatal sexuality, an interpretive dead end that makes film noir nihilist in a way that is belied by the profound and variegated interest these films hold for viewers and critics.

3
Psychological Disorders and "Wiretapping the Unconscious": Film Noir Listens to Women

In Chapter 1, I referenced the hard-boiled Ethel Whitehead from *The Damned Don't Cry*, who says, "You gotta kick and punch and belt your way up cuz nobody's going to give you a lift." The language of kicking and punching as a response to the exigencies of modern life echoes Annie Laurie's demands in Joseph Lewis's *Gun Crazy*, released, interestingly, in 1950, the same year as was *The Damned Don't Cry*. Says Annie Laurie (Peggy Cummins), "I've been kicked around all my life. From now on, I'm going to kick back." In one of the most memorable moments of the film, Bart asks Annie Laurie, "Why do you kill?" in that tone of strangely untethered questioning that David Lynch would rehearse in *Blue Velvet* (1986), when Jeffrey Beaumont asks, "Why are there people like Frank Booth?" Annie Laurie's answer to Bart belies her canonic status as evil "femme fatale." She says, "I do it because I'm afraid. I panic," suggesting a portrait of desperation or mental illness: a young woman who experiences life as a hunted animal. As Adrian Martin says, Annie Laurie "shoots to kill whenever fear overwhelms her; whenever she is seized hysterically by the threat of loss" (84). The tone of Martin's essay is personal, but its content seems to me right, in the sense that it doesn't cast Annie Laurie simply as a "femme fatale" but suggests the desperation of her needs and desires and her passion for and devotion, within those terms, to Bart.

In this regard, Martin rightly points to the scene in which both Annie Laurie and Bart escape their big heist only to run back to each other in a passionate and mutual embrace. The movie is anti-bourgeois, against the model of marriage presented, as Martin says, by Bart's sister and her "dreary nuclear family" (84). Jim Kitses also takes a more sympathetic view of Annie Laurie, reading her in the context of postwar gender anxiety ("[Annie Laurie] signifies the complex questions surrounding gender and role that arose in the social upheaval of post-war America" [49]) and an anger derived from a futile desire for excitement and independence. Laurie has a "rage born of life under men, life needful of men" (61). More than just having ambitions beyond conventional gender and social roles, as I discussed in my last chapter, some notable women in noir express trauma, rebellion, and anger as madness.

In *Gun Crazy* Bart and Laurie both take up the language of ambition voiced by Cora in *The Postman Always Rings Twice*, Annie Laurie insisting to Bart, "I want things. I want a lot of things." From the beginning of the film, Bart feels that his gun gives him agency, addressing his desire to "be somebody": "I've just got to have a gun . . . shooting's what I'm good at. It's the only thing I like. It's what I want to do when I grow up." This parody of the American Dream, Laurie's and Bart's perverse response to alienation, "resonates," as Kitses notes, "in the American Psyche" (32). When he shoots, Bart says, "I feel awful good inside, like I'm somebody."

Bart and Laurie violate every law but that of human passion, and *Gun Crazy*'s fascination with these outsiders' "craze" serves to question the viability and, indeed, the sustainability, of a conventional regulation of desires. Annie Laurie's self-righteous boss Miss Sifert, played as the "old bitty" Laurie calls her, chastises Laurie for wearing pants to work and goads Laurie into shooting by pulling the burglar alarm. More pointedly, the film portrays Bart's sister Ruby Tare as trapped in domesticity. Ruby is vacant of passion or energy. She's a run-down, worn-out baby-maker and housekeeper, whose husband's absence is marked in the film.

Presaging Hitchcock's representation of the carnival's lawlessness in *Strangers on a Train* by one year, the fairgrounds venue in *Gun Crazy* functions in pointed contrast to the ordered and depressing life of Ruby Tare. This point is well demonstrated in the lack of establishing shots before Lewis's sudden cut to Annie's and Bart's exciting roller coaster ride (Figure 3.1).

As Kitses says, the carnival has a "function in catering to humanity's hunger for release, its need to escape the everyday, to lose one's self" (25).

The movies I address in this chapter figure women expressing through madness an aggressive response to social rules that belittle them. The female psychoses represented in these films invite sympathy for female confinement and desperation. The tone of these films strongly suggests sympathy toward the bizarre and subversive ways in which these women respond to their situations, which are presented very often as traumatic.

Referring to Annie Laurie's and Bart's desperate slog through the forest at the end of *Gun Crazy* (Figure 3.2) ("Let them come," Annie Laurie says; "I kill them! I kill them!"), Kitses says, "[Annie] Laurie's fear is traumatic, her loss of

Figure 3.1 Bart (John Dall) and Annie Laurie (Peggy Cummins) on the roller coaster in *Gun Crazy* (1950) BFI. *Gun Crazy* © Pioneer Pictures Corporation. Licensed By: Warner Bros. Entertainment Inc. All Rights Reserved.

Figure 3.2 Trapped in the forest: Bart (John Dall) and Annie Laurie (Peggy Cummins) in *Gun Crazy* (1950) BFI. *Gun Crazy* © Pioneer Pictures Corporation. Licensed By: Warner Bros. Entertainment Inc. All Rights Reserved.

self total. It is possible to see in moments such as these Laurie's own victimization, her aggression a logical response to hard, damaging life" (61).

The painful close-ups of Annie Laurie at the end of the film, as well as the fury of her defiance of the town's "nice-guy" authority figures, Sheriff Clyde and Newsman Dave (who are bringing the dogs after Bart and Laurie), support a reading of her as damaged, desperate, crazed, and sympathetic: "Let them come! I kill them! I kill them!" The example suggests not only the ways in which film noir movies rebel against normative representations of women, but also the extent to which dangerous women in noir are presented as sympathetic and traumatized rather than opaque figures of destruction. While the crazy women of noir often fall easily into the category of "femme fatale," as it has been internalized by viewers and critics, these women in particular defy the grounds of conventional gender roles. Movies like *Leave her to Heaven* (1945), *Possessed* (1947), *Whirlpool* (1949), *Gun Crazy* (1950), and *Sunset Boulevard* (1950) (which I'll address more fully in the final chapter) portray women who seem insane—but all of these films also portray the limited possibilities on offer for the modern woman, the ways in which social institutions like family and marriage, and Hollywood as well (in the case of *Sunset Boulevard*) sap women's energy and relegate them to gendered prisons, such prisons often cast as the ostensibly safe zones of normative domestic life. It makes sense, then, that one way to attack these norms is to present women or the spheres that entrap them as patently unsafe. The women in these films are, in narrative terms, mentally unstable, but their instability reflects a rebellion against patriarchal rules that not only deny them value in psychosocial realms but that make them crazy, ready to act and react violently to the authority figures and patriarchal institutions that govern their lives.

Possessed (1947), the film Joan Crawford made after *Mildred Pierce*, portrays a woman's sanity as the cost of modernity. In *Possessed*, Louise's ambition to have a meaningful life that is valued by others and over which she has some control has driven her to psychosis. The film makes clear that class and gender are not only the source of but, further, even define Louise's illness.

Louise Howell, played by Crawford, arrives at the "psychopathic department" of the hospital in what is diagnosed as a "catatonic stupor." The social environment of the film, established by the two doctors attending to Louise, is expressed in terms of rampant mental illness. Indeed, as Louise is wheeled in for observation, Dr. Willard asks, "How many does this make?" The other attending doctor replies "Twenty today: one maniac; three seniles; six alcoholics; and ten schitzos." The setting of mental trauma is very notably defined as female. Dr. Willard's accounting of "beautiful

Figure 3.3   Louise Howell (Joan Crawford) in a "catatonic stupor" in *Possessed* (1947), while her attending doctors discuss the case. George Eastman House. *Possessed* © Turner Entertainment Co. A Warner Bros. Entertainment Company. All Rights Reserved.

women . . . talented . . . frustrated" points to an inability of the *femme moderne* to thrive, finding the source of this failure to be a sick society: "This civilization of ours," says Dr. Willard, "is the worst disease." About Louise, Dr. Willard intones, "Frustrated, just like all the others" (Figure 3.3).

"The others" populate the film too. Pauline Grahame has paranoid fantasies about her husband having an affair with Nurse Louise and eventually ends her torment in suicide. Pauline is an invalid, trapped in mental illness like Bertha Mason, *Jane Eyre*'s "madwoman in the attic." Louise is nurse to Pauline; after Pauline dies, Louise is governess, like Jane Eyre at Thornfield, to her child. In the Grahame household, Louise feels herself to be, as Jane Eyre describes her experience at the Lowood School, "an inmate of its walls." Jane craves freedom ("I desired liberty; for liberty I gasped; for liberty I uttered a prayer" [Bronte, 86]), as Louise makes clear she does too, in her impassioned speech to Dean Grahame (Raymond Massey, admittedly no Rochester) when she decides to leave her job as nanny to young Wynn Grahame after Pauline dies. When Dean comments, "You're usually so quiet," Louise replies:

Yes, quiet, patient Miss Howell. Tell her to do something and she does it, day after day, year after year, and at the age of sixty, she retires with a gold watch and the blessings of the entire household. Oh, no thank you. I've had enough of being a servant.

The quote echoes Jane's desire for something more than "the routine of eight years in one afternoon," as Jane says of her time at Lowood (86). More pointedly, just as Jane, eager to leave Lowood, famously exclaims, "Grant me at least a new servitude," Louise searches for new venues for her ambition and desire, which are mostly sublimated into efficient Victorian feminine role-playing on the one hand and destructive and utterly misplaced obsessive regard for David Sutton (Van Heflin) on the other. In the end, we see Louise shoot bounder Sutton, but the murdering female figure is presented throughout *Possessed* as a woman trapped in modern patriarchy, where she lives to serve or is alternately disregarded by selfish and cynical David Sutton.

Louise, like Mildred Pierce, is overinvested—here, in romantic love rather than motherhood. Louise's obsession with her caddish lover Sutton represents a perverse expression of a desire that is keyed to social realities Joan Crawford and other strong and intelligent women in post-war America were keenly aware of. According to Buszek

> Joan Crawford, for example, became the era's icon for the steely self-reliance and ambition of the Depression-era actress largely because of how fanzine discourse seized upon her real-life (and still infamous) battles for success in Hollywood. Her struggles were held up against those of *Photoplay*'s readership when the magazine assured them that Crawford has "taken hard knocks. She's been broke and miserable, as many worthwhile people have been."
>
> (188)

When *Mildred Pierce* was released in 1945, the film's press materials incorporated her "difficult journey" into promotion of the film's emphasis on female ambition: "[Crawford's] intense approach to any problem startles many people. Nevertheless, it is unquestionably the answer to how she climbed the ladder of success and how she stays on top" (*Mildred Pierce* Press book, BFI). The article, "Actress's Rise to Film Stardom Was Difficult Journey," recounts Crawford's graduation from being on call for "leg art," to her huge success at MGM. Crawford's eventual refusal to take what she considered "trite" roles led to her break with MGM before her comeback, or "return," as Norma Desmond would have it, in Warner Brothers' production of *Mildred Pierce*: "She came up the hard way, earning her success."

Possessed, released on the heels of *Mildred Pierce*'s success and Joan Crawford's academy-award-winning performance in the earlier film, represents Louise already in crisis, as the film begins. After the initial scene discussed above in which Louise roams the streets of Washington DC looking for "David," landing in the psychiatric ward of the hospital, Louise tells her story, and the film flashes back to narrate her romance with David Sutton. Interestingly, however, the film never presents an initial or satisfying part of their relationship, an earlier time when the love affair between Louise and David Sutton was presumably going well. From the moment we flash back to their relationship, Louise is pushing romance, and David seems bored and distracted (Figure 3.4). "You're not even listening to me," Louise says. Romance is deflated further with Louise's ironic response to David's silence when she asks him, "Do you love me?" When David fails to answer, Louise says, "You say the most beautiful things." His eventual response, "I like all kinds of music except a little number called 'Oh Promise Me,'" then "it's a duet, and I like to play solo," shows him to be self-satisfied and uninterested in Louise.

Also deflating the romance plot, the film presents Louise fairly immediately as desperate ("I can never lose you"), while David insists, "You're choking me to death."

Figure 3.4 Louise Howell (Joan Crawford) and David Sutton (Van Heflin) in *Possessed* (1947) George Eastman House. *Possessed* © Turner Entertainment Co. A Warner Bros. Entertainment Company. All Rights Reserved.

Still, Louise presents a case for herself, always having lived "on the outside": "I can't go back being on the outside of people's lives looking in." There's a strange resonance of women's postwar deprivation in this scene, which could serve as a microcosm of the making of the "femme fatale." Formerly voyeurs, as it were, women were on the outside before the war; during World War II, women were invited to participate in social production: "the active female character [in such films as *Phantom Lady*] coincided with a homefront audience of working wartime women" (Biesen, 166). Forced to resume exclusively conventional roles of wives and mothers after the war, women were forced to relinquish their passion for more varied experience, for participating in society. As Shema Bermer Gluck notes, "The sexual division of labor, never totally eliminated during the war, became firmly entrenched again after the war, and many women were forced back into lower-paying female dominated occupations"(17).

In *Possessed*, Louise won't relinquish her passionate side. Being forced to do so (notably by a man who is cynical and debauched) drives her to insanity ("something happens to a woman," she later tells David, "when she isn't wanted"), becoming, at the end of the film, after struggling and suffering throughout its narrative, a killer. She shoots David Sutton, who shows increasing contempt for her attachment to him. She trades her supplication for anger when he says to her, "[w]hen a woman kisses me, she has to take pot luck."

While at certain points Louise shows anger and deception, at other points, she's nurturing and kind and shows intelligence about society and human relationships that centers her as our point of identification in the film. That Louise is our point of identification the film makes clear at the beginning in an extended point-of-view tracking shot, bringing us into Louise's experience on a literal and visceral level, as the camera records her view of the hospital ceilings in low-angle shots when she is wheeled into the emergency room. The film's sympathy for Louise is also seen in her earnest care of young Wynn Grahame, as well as her concern for Wynn's father Dean, which drives her to visit his daughter Carol at school to explain her relationship with Dean.

Louise struggles to find contentment, which she seems to find with kindly Dean Grahame. However, David Sutton keeps reappearing, resurrecting Louise's self-loathing and loathing of David. This desperation reaches its peak when David and Carol Grahame begin a romance, prompting Louise's murder of David and repeating the perverse mother/daughter/cad lover triangle presented in *Mildred Pierce*.

At the hospital, Louise's "problem" is named in clunky 40s American pop culture Freudianism as a "classic" persecution complex, and schizophrenia. She loses her ability to distinguish between reality and fantasy, her senses betray her, and she resorts to violence. At one point, the film presents Louise upset by her stepdaughter Carol taunting her with her own affair with David: Louise throws Carol down the stairs (we see Geraldine Fitzgerald tumble down the stairs), but then the image of Carol dissolves, and we realize the assault was a fantasy. Two points need to be observed about these oneiric scenes, enhanced here by German émigré Curtis Bernhardt's expressionist filmmaking. On the one hand, the dream sequences and the focus on fantasy complement a theme presented in this and other noir films of the difficulties for modern men and women to separate projection and fantasy from reality. Through the noir viewpoint, such projection and fantasy are a cultural habit particularly destructive as they inform gender conventions. On the other hand, the continual shifting of narrative grounds in *Possessed* effectively circumvents our own projections and judgments onto the narrative. For example, we learn only after Carol tumbles down the stairs and she and Louise fight viciously that this is Louise's fantasy. The film surprises us again later when Louise admits that she took Pauline down to the dock and was responsible for her death. We take Louise's tortured admission at face value (since the film never shows Pauline's suicide, until Dean responds to the confession, insisting and providing evidence for the fact that it is delusion and, again, Louise's fantasy).

Such undermining of our knowledge about the terms of the narrative presents a challenge to viewers to expand their frame of reference in interpreting narrative and image. The film's investment in blurring the lines that divide reality and fantasy may speak to the dangers of the break between the real and the imaginary when fantasy and projection shut down empathy and higher-order thinking, but the merger of fantasies and reality also demands a more productive openness in our response to narrative and representation, a theme central to Preminger's *Whirlpool* and, as I will argue in my last chapter, to David Lynch's *Mulholland Drive*. In *Possessed*, David Sutton's preference for mathematics over love—"two and two are always four, and that's wonderful"—is judged by the film to be a failed and cynical rejection of the need for understanding and extending sympathy toward human desire and the extreme distress often associated with it.

Louise, at the end of *Possessed*, is said to have endured "great emotional strain." She has a "tortured mind," and she is "possessed of devils." No happy ending beyond is forecast, since "it's pain that made her this way." The doctor tells Dean Grahame that she will endure "suffering beyond belief." *Possessed* presents the story of a woman often read simply as a "femme fatale"—Eddie Muller misidentifies the tone of the film when he refers to how Louise "destroys Van Heflin, even though he's the love of her life" (61)—who is complex, varied, and victimized by convention and patriarchy.

Like *Possessed*, *Leave Her to Heaven* is concerned with the psychosocial pressures on women that make them sick. The film was made in color, unusual for a 1945 film noir movie. In this film, Ellen Berent, played by Gene Tierney, falls in love with Dick Harland (Cornel Wilde), a writer she meets on the train. Ellen's possessiveness over Dick and her need for control culminate in the memorable scene in which she takes Dick's crippled little brother Danny for a swim in the lake, leaving the boy to drown in the cold waters, while she looks impassively on, calmly repeating, "You can do it. Swim to the boat, Danny. You can do it." The perversity of the scene—the brutal murder of a young disabled boy—is as overdetermined as is Ellen's overattachment to Dick generally, providing an opportunity for viewers to wonder what the source of Ellen's sickness is.

Clearly what's in part in play in this film is a scrutiny of the boring existence of middle-class morality, here the color of the film functioning, with Ellen, as a gesture of vitality in a black and white conventional setting. Ellen's feeling of being trapped in a family vice is starkly portrayed in a morning bedroom scene, in which Ellen's and Dick's romance is interrupted by the rapping on the wall by Danny: "Hey! Good morning! How 'bout a swim?" That Dick is oblivious to the intrusion and to his wife's annoyance constitutes his status as a "dumb lug" in the film (to borrow from the title of B. Ruby Rich's 1995 *Sight and Sound* article). This is most directly portrayed in Dick's meandering around the lake whistling while his brother drowns, a scene like Vargas's driving by the balcony from which Susan desperately shouts in *Touch of Evil* (1958); Vargas is oblivious to her screams above, symbolizing the male imperviousness to the trauma and perversity that characterizes the social worlds delineated in film noir. In *Leave Her to Heaven*, Ellen's annoyance at intrusion, while in part signifying her psychotic possessiveness over Dick, is also seen when the Robies arrive on the boat to visit. While the film provides a long shot of the Robies on the boat waving happily at Ellen and Dick, the film cuts to Ellen's reaction, which is perversely unfriendly and annoyed. Seen through Ellen's anti-bourgeois perspective, this scene, like the one in which Danny raps on the bedroom walls—and even the one in which poor Danny drowns while

Ellen looks coldly on—plays almost parodically, drawing attention to the absurd clashing of worlds—Ellen's perversity and desire; Dick's, the Berents', and the Robies' blank conventionality.

Ellen's violent rebellion against middle-class values can also be seen in her battle with maternity. Caught between wanting Dick to herself and wanting to make him happy through conventional means—having a baby—she cannot cope with the burdens of pregnancy: "This baby's making a prisoner of me. I can't do anything, can't go anywhere. I hate the little beast. I wish it would die." That the burden is figured in terms of imprisonment is interesting, suggesting that Ellen's madness is at least in part a result of the cognitive disjunction resulting from her own powers and desires bumping up against the demands of convention, expectation, and "expecting."

The film symbolizes Ellen's power in intriguing ways. She appropriates not only the male gaze as she stares at Dick on the train, but also the conventional male prerogative of proposing matrimony—"Darling, will you marry me?" The film references her powerful will over Danny (ironically, it is Ellen to whom Danny's improvement is attributed—Dr. Mason says to her, "You must have willed that boy to walk").

There are, additionally, references to Ellen as a "witch." At their initial meeting on the train, Dick says in response to Ellen knowing all about him (from the book jacket), "If you'd lived in Salem years ago, they would have burned you." The idea of the supernatural is evoked again in Ellen's appearance, after her swim, as she rises up from the waters like a sea beast to greet Dick.

Such figuration of Ellen is not so much a standard tapping into the "femme fatale" role but a portrait of female power as perverse, when it is forced into a conventional mold of social roles and expectations. An example of this is the commentary on Ellen's competitiveness, which is judged and made to seem eerie by Glen Robie. As Ellen races Lynn in the lake, Dick says to Glen, "Lynn's going to win," and Robie says, "No. Ellen. Ellen always wins." The tone of fatalism here reflects, again, female power as perverse. Ellen's final powerful gesture is the ultimate in perversity, since she poisons herself to frame her rival, the woman (contrasting with Ellen) associated throughout the film with nature and the natural, "The Girl with the Hoe" ("Ruth Berent," Ellen's adopted sister and cousin, played by Jeanne Crain).

On a certain level, any viewer must acknowledge that Ellen *is* crazy. My point here is not that Ellen is a positive role model for women, or even that she is herself feminist, or that she isn't crazy. My point is, rather, that the film, like most film noir movies, provides a context for her action that complicates a simple reading of Ellen as "femme fatale." One context for understanding Ellen, I should add, must be the gender expectations of audience members that 20th Century Fox sought to capitalize on in strange ways. The film's Press book (BFI) offers one suggestion to exhibitors of *Leave Her to Heaven*, exploiting unflattering views of women to promote the film: "Plant the following letter," Fox suggests to theaters, "on your local woman's page, pointing out to the editor its interesting possibilities as a peg for a feature story, feature article, editorial, or letter-writing contest!" Here is the rather stunning letter Fox proposes to plant:

> Dear Miss . . . . . :
>
> Last night I saw the picture "Leave Her to Heaven" at the . . . Theatre, and to a young, eligible male who spent three years overseas away, for the most part, from feminine companionship, the theme of the picture certainly gave me a great deal to think about before marrying and settling down to a "calm," happy existence with any one woman.
> It may be that the heroine of the picture was a bit exaggerated in her fanatical insistence that her husband devote all of his attention and affection to her, and her alone. I know, too, that a husband is expected to show some allegiance to the woman he marries. But from what I hear of the demands being made by girls today, the picture can't be very far off.
> Just how much should a fellow getting married today be expected to give up in the way of independence? And equally important, how much in the way of a monopoly on her husband's every thought and action has a girl the right to demand? I'd like to know before I even begin a half-way serious search for a lifetime companion.
>   Puzzled Bachelor
> *Girls, what do you think?*

The planted editorial ends with this teaser appeal to popular audiences, exploiting biased gender assumptions that overshadow the film's subtlety.

I take this film, and the others I discuss in this chapter as examples, because in one sense they are the most extreme illustrations of "fatal" women; however, as I'm suggesting, the very extremity of the actions of these women redounds on the social institutions that propel them to psychotic behavior. Since these characters are representations rather than models of what women (or men, for that matter) should emulate in "real" life, it behooves us to come to a finer understanding of how these figures interact with and respond to the social settings that in part define their actions.

In Chapter 2, I referenced Scott Snyder, who has classified the "femme fatale" in clinical psychological terms. In his essay, "Personality Disorder and the *Film Noir Femme Fatale*," Snyder explores the ways in which "femmes fatales" reflect "Cluster B" personality disorders.[1] While I'm intrigued by the effort to contextualize the portrayal of women in noir in behaviorist psychological terms, especially in this essay's exploration of postwar gender anxiety and its relevance to the representation of women in noir, the schematic superimposition of DSM categories on particular female characters results in misreadings and further objectification of female experience as "Other." While in the following passage Snyder means to follow up his claim that the "femme fatale" is a misogynist projection, his employment of Eddie Muller's commentary on "the femme fatale" itself projects Muller's ideation onto "real" psychological cases.

> "[W]omen break out of the molds cast for them in the rigid spiritual and social structures of the ruling patriarchy. There's no greater kick in this town than when a woman finally wraps her delicate fingers around the trigger of a .38 Linga and blasts away every bit of genetic encoding and cultural repression in a roaring fusillade of little lead forget-me-nots" (Muller, 1998). She epitomizes the Cluster B personality disorder (Synder, 159).

I've already discussed the troubling habit of criticism and popular culture to unquestioningly adopt the language of the "femme fatale," but here we see a good example of the disturbing "real-life" effects of such wide-scale projection, when professional psychologists like Dr. Snyder are weaving the type, the "femme fatale," into the fabric of the disciplines, in this case, psychotherapy.

A use of the discipline of psychology allowing for greater nuance might invoke the work of Marsha Linehan, whose clinical research has shown that women with borderline personalities have a history of living within "an invalidating environment," defined as "one in which communication of private experiences is met by erratic, inappropriate, and extreme responses. In other words, the expression of private experiences is not validated; instead, it is often punished and/or trivialized" (49). While Linehan's work is clinically based and refers to invalidating environments in individuals' case histories, Linehan's studies resonate in the context of social history and the acculturation of gender roles. Linehan's analysis provides a useful frame for a discussion of noir's women, who are striking out, sometimes pathologically, as a result of having no context in which their actions have real meaning or purpose.

Women who aren't validated, for Linehan, can panic and act out in severe ways: "much of the borderline behavior that is interpreted as stemming from hostile motives and anger stems in reality from fear, panic, hopelessness, and desperation" (70). Linehan's insights have a resonance when we discuss the "panicked" women in noir, who feel trapped and desperate and are often shown to be reacting against patriarchal norms and conventions that stifle their creativity and independence. These kinds of portraits are not limited to those that appear in Hollywood melodrama, or "women's films," as I suggested in Chapter 1. The representation of women caged in social roles is also significantly present in film noir, a point elided by a preoccupation with the idea that women in noir are defined in terms of the "good girl" and the "femme fatale."

Linehan also makes a point analogous to the one I made in the last chapter about female independence being perceived differently from male independence (the latter a mark of strength, the former a sign of perversity). The poles of dependence and independence are valued differently, in gendered terms:

> What happens to women who either are not given the social support they need or are taught that their very need for social support is itself unhealthy. . . . Feminine characteristics such as interpersonal dependence and relying on others—which, as noted above, are positively related to women's mental health—are generally perceived as mentally "unhealthy" (Widgier and Settle, 1987). We so value independence that we apparently cannot conceive of the possibility that a person could have too much independence. For example, although there is a "dependent personality disorder" in the DSM-IV, there is no "independent personality disorder."
>
> (55)

Linehan's point here helps us to understand why some of the "homme fatales" discussed in the last chapter, whose extremity is read in terms of radical independence rather than pathology, don't shatter norms but merely extend an accepted code of masculinity that bulwarks rather than undermines conventional expectations.

The application of Linehan's work to representations of noir can broaden our understanding of what is being represented rather than reinforcing categories belied by careful textual analysis. For example, Snyder discusses the mirror images that recur in film noir, keying these scenes to the films' suggestion of female narcissism, a further sign of the films' misogyny, in the terms of Snyder's argument:

> The independence which *film noir* women seek is often visually presented as self-absorbed narcissism: the woman gazes at her own reflection in the mirror, ignoring the man she will use to achieve her goals. The self-absorption of Phyllis Dietrichson occurs in numerous scenes in *Double Indemnity* (1944). The "mirror shots" also indicate women's duplicitous nature: they are visually split, thus not to be trusted. The mirror motif also contributes to the murky confusion of *film noir*: nothing and no one is what it seems.

Snyder references Phyllis Dietrichson here, supporting my point in Chapter 1 that criticism most invested in maintaining the category of the "femme fatale" repeatedly falls back on Phyllis Dietrichson and two or three other women in noir whose motives are opaque.[2] More important, while the last part of Snyder's comment is surely right—that mirrors, like other visual icons in film noir, such as fog and cigarette smoke, and chiaroscuro shadows, suggest the obscurity of moral choices and of meaning more generally—in the context of female mental illness, such mirrors can just as easily be read as screens from which women ask for validation and respect. If it is true, as Linehan's research has shown, that personality disorders are directly linked to validation and affirmation in women's lives, then the preoccupation with mirrors in film noir can easily be connected to female characters' sense of their own superfluidity and lack of value. Mirrors also represent one's presence in reverse, as its opposite, which suggests a value in questioning the presentation and interpretation of selfhood and image. Debbie Marsh stares at herself repeatedly in *The Big Heat*, but she is also driven in the film to find meaning in her life beyond the role she has had as Vince Stone's moll. She does finally elicit respect from Detective Bannion, but not until she has sacrificed her life, quite heroically indeed, to bring down "the big heat" and get rid of the city's network of thugs and gangsters.

Otto Preminger's 1949 film *Whirlpool* is an intriguing example of a woman's personality disorder reflecting her need for validation. Given that the film is about the inner conflicts of Ann Sutton (Gene Tierney), it's interesting that the film begins by referencing post-World War II trauma, conventionally associated with male anxiety (as is explored in Krutnik's *In a Lonely Street*). In an early scene in *Whirlpool*, Ann's husband Bill (Richard Conte), an acclaimed psychoanalyst, reports to Ann about a client of his, a veteran, who has stopped talking: "It's difficult to begin unloading fears and secrets and guilts. . . . Poor fellow. The war was an easier conflict than the one he's in now."

The trauma the film focuses on, however, is Ann's. Her kleptomania, which she keeps secret from her revered husband, reflects her resistance to unnatural and oppressive roles she must play as a woman, shifting the standard focus of postwar trauma on men to the gender chaos the postwar period introduced for women.[3] Perhaps signifying women's dislocation (not just men's) after the men returned from the war and resumed their positions in the workplace (thus pushing women back into the home), Ann Sutton's kleptomania is linked not only to feeling trapped in a role as the trophy-wife of her famous husband, but also to the restrictions placed on her by her father when she was a child, when she first started stealing. The film goes on to explore issues central to the representation of women in film noir: women craving expression and independence; female rebellion against patriarchal rules, institutions, and individuals for not acknowledging or respecting female desire and ambition; and the deadly expectation that women will deceive and lie. That women in noir are victimized by the last of these themes and sympathized with for their role in connection with the first and second themes has been a fundamental assumption on which this project is based.

The points are aptly made in *Whirlpool*. In the film, it is fairly quickly established that Ann yearns for more meaning in her life and a more significant role in her marriage. She agitates to her husband for a more meaningful role in her marriage, at the same time as her comments suggest her low self-esteem: "I just wish that I could help you—if I were only brighter and you could talk to me about your scientific problems." Ann's role in the marriage is limited to how she reflects on Bill, who says to her, "Just stay as you are, as you've always been—healthy and adorable." A little later in the film, he boasts:

> You know the greatest kick I get when we go to a party together is when people stare at you and say, "Who is that lovely girl. Why that's Dr. Sutton's wife. She's very devoted to him." My head swells up like a balloon.

The film perfectly exemplifies Linehan's delineation of the "nonacceptance or oversimplification" of the female subject in the case of borderline personality. Ann is utterly isolated, and her desire to have some meaningful role to play is, in Linehan's terms, "unaccepted" and "oversimplified." Underscoring Ann's isolation is the lack of a social network for Ann: no friends and no family are represented in the film; as Richard Schickel points out in his audio commentary of *Whirlpool*, Ann's social support is "notably absent."

The film goes a long way toward directly linking Bill's treatment of her with her "sickness," Ann finally shouting at the police station, as she is tested, like Laura in Tierney's previous film with Otto Preminger, under high-angle shots and the unsympathetic lights of police interrogation: "[Korvo] didn't unbalance me or drive me to anything. Bill did." Then, to Bill, she says:

> Run away from the truth as you have ever since you married me! You made me playact! I had to pretend I was healthy and happy when I was sick and miserable! Headaches. I couldn't sleep; afraid to tell you, afraid to lose your wonderful love!

This language of "playacting" has admittedly been used earlier by the villainous Korvo (Jose Ferrer), who exploits Ann, hypnotizing her so that he is able to frame her for the murder of Theresa Randolph. Still, that the searing anti-bourgeois social criticism is first issued forth by the film's criminal doesn't mitigate the film's sympathy for the position outlined by Korvo and for Ann Sutton's victimization by the men around her and their smug and false assumptions about her motives and her behavior.

While Korvo is a crazed killer and exploiter, he is right that Ann was living within a "torture chamber called Mrs. William Sutton," the psychological prison that prodded her to rebel by breaking the law, returning to her earlier habit of stealing. It is noteworthy that Ann explains her kleptomania as deriving from her father's control over her:

> I did it before. I stole, in school, when my father wouldn't let me spend money. And even after he died. He tied it all up in a trust fund. Thousands and thousands of dollars, but I could never have a new dress, or have anything I wanted. That's how I fooled my father, by stealing. He didn't love me. He thought he did but he didn't. Nobody ever caught me. I thought it was over when I left school and met Bill . . . it came back because he was like my father. He treated me like my father did. And I had to do it again. I tried not to.

Bill later explains that he, like Ann's father, controlled her through money, insisting when they married that she not use any of her inheritance. An invalidating environment and unconcern about Ann's desires, defined here in social economic terms, causes her rebellion. The control of her father and of Bill are, in psychoanalytic terms, presented at the beginning of the film, when we are introduced to Bill by way of the name plate on his front door, "William Sutton, MD," establishing Bill's absent presence, "the law of the father," as an authority in Ann's life.

One of the main identifying features of the fatal woman, as she is discussed in film criticism, is her deceptiveness. The lack of trust placed in women is not only an issue of failing to validate female identity (in Linehan's terms) but is also in film noir often the source of destruction. It is, in other words, the men's mistrust of women that causes problems. In *Whirlpool*, the men fail the challenge offered to them to rely on their unscientific understanding rather than legal reasoning. As in Jake Gittes's fatal mistrust of Evelyn Mulwray, the men around Ann don't have the imaginative understanding to discern Ann's innocence. That this is a major problem the film suggests in its obsessiveness with the idea of truth and lying, accentuated by the plot's concern with psychoanalysis and hypnosis. When she realizes that Bill, the lawyer, and the lieutenant don't believe her, Ann cries desperately, "You won't believe me! You think I'm lying! . . . You don't believe me!" The change from predictive to descriptive—from "you won't believe me" to "you don't believe me"—suggests a fatalism to Ann's cry here: that the men can't, like Othello, see beyond the physical and the evidentiary. Othello accords too much meaning to (assumes an affair with Cassio from seeing) Desdemona's handkerchief, just as the men cannot come to terms with Ann's fingerprints in Korvo's apartment. (While Korvo plants a glass with Ann's fingerprints on it in his apartment, Ann insists she has not entered Korvo's hotel apartment.) The fingerprints seem to "prove" that Ann is lying—says Bill, "You were there. There's proof. You can't sit there and deny a love affair that's known to everyone—to the police, to me, to a hundred witnesses." Bill is guided by ratiocination and a wounded ego, rather than by caring for Ann. He is, throughout most of the film, a "dumb lug," unable to extend Ann imaginative sympathy. His lack of faith in Ann is pointed to by Korvo, who speaks the truth when he says, "Poor Ann: in jail, in real danger, and you bellowing with wounded vanity."

Bill's failed sympathy and insight rehearses a masculinist approach to experience, one illuminated by Susan Glaspell in her 1917 short story "A Jury of Her Peers." As in "A Jury of Her Peers," the men and their imperviousness to female desire and subjectivity, as well as their rationalist reading of experience, are the source of female misery. Glaspell's short story, *Whirlpool*, and, I believe, film noir generally, explore the different varieties of crimes committed in the modern world as a result of gender categorization and division. The men in Glaspell's short story dismiss Mrs. Hale's and Mrs. Peter's work in the kitchen as "trifles," an assertion of hierarchal gender ordering that moves the women to protect Minnie Wright, who had married Mr. Wright, a hard man, who was "like a raw wind that gets to the bone" (188). While their husbands fruitlessly search the house for physical clues to the murder, Mrs. Hale and Mrs. Peters (the latter, the sheriff's wife, initially described as "married to the law") remain in the kitchen and gradually discover proof of Mrs. Wright's murder of her husband, as well as a motive, when they find the bird symbolizing Minnie Wright's vitality and mental freedom killed by Mr. Wright's hand. Thus the women solve the crime: Mrs. Wright gave up. "A person," says Mrs. Peters, "gets discouraged and loses heart" (185), and Minnie Wright killed her husband.

Through their intuitive cooperative leadership, Mrs. Hale and Mrs. Peters then decide as active social agents to cover the crime up to protect Minnie Wright, establishing higher-order values in empathy and in rebellion against male brutality (Mr. Wright) and condescension (the men in the house with Mrs. Hale and Mrs. Peters). Further, the workings of logic, extolled by the smug sheriff and lawyers in Glaspell's story, are seen not only as a lower-order value but also as impotent, since, to the end, the men maintain that the women are in the kitchen engaging in "trifles." As in Glaspell's short story, in *Whirlpool*, the men's gender assumptions about Ann blind them to her plight. Failing to extend beyond rationalist approaches to problem-solving, the men fail Ann.

Interestingly, the villainous David Korvo does not share the scientific approach to knowledge. He relies, in contrast to the other men in the film, on irrationalist hypnosis. While Schickel notes that Korvo is "right" in his analysis of Ann's problem, that she is being suffocated by her "suburban, bland, unengaging existence" (Schickel), he (Schickel, that is) doesn't draw conclusions about Korvo's correct diagnosis. Korvo may be a "rogue" and a "fraud" (and is obviously a killer too) and a "master manipulator," but his "irrationalist" account of Ann's troubles is more truthful than the men's crude application of reason and rationality. Korvo's reference to the tools of psychoanalysis, taping analysands (as Sutton does to Theresa Randolph during their sessions), "wiretapping the unconscious," speaks with more resonance to the film's interest in different kinds of knowing.

Ann's illness is a register of the social pathology of her world, including the hyperrationalist fact-seekers in the Lieutenant and the lawyer and Bill

Sutton, her husband the psychoanalyst. Like John the doctor-husband in Charlotte Perkins Gilman's "The Yellow Wallpaper," who insists that the female protagonist is fine and that there is nothing "medically," or factually wrong with her ("[John] knows there is no *reason* to suffer, and that satisfies him" [Gilman, 44]), the men in *Whirlpool* mistake an evidentiary mode of knowing for the truth, and further drive the victim-heroine into despair. That the stakes of this battle between understanding and sympathy on the one hand and fact-based conventional knowing on the other are high is clear in Tierney's performance in the police station scenes. Here, Ann is shown to be panicked by the gradual understanding that she is helpless to combat the evidence applied to her case by circumstances and rational explanations (as quoted above, "You won't believe me! You think I'm lying! . . . You don't believe me!").

Here, I think it's important to note that the film undermines the hermeneutics of knowability that so often undergird the reading of women in noir. On the one hand, knowing Ann—analyzing her using rationalist evidentiary techniques—victimizes her and fails to attain truth. On the other hand, the myth of unknowability is in play here, although mainly brought to bear by critics. Schickel talks about the "troubled enigmatic figures" in the Fox quintet, enigmatic characters like Ann and Laura, both of whom are in fact misinterpreted and wrongly grilled under the police-investigative so-called light of reason. Further, Schickel elides the boundary between character and actress (an interpretive habit discussed in the previous chapter), noting that Gene Tierney was the "resident somnambulist" at Fox, adding to the myth of enigmatic woman that redounds on the women she portrays. Some contemporary film reviews assessed Tierney similarly, the *Monthly Film Bulletin* suggesting that while Jose Ferrer is a compelling villain, "Gene Tierney is less successful, it being sometimes difficult to detect from her playing whether she is or is not under hypnosis." Careful examination of the film reveals a strong woman who is, in whatever ways she can manage in the face of resistance, trying to liberate herself from the bonds of patriarchy and convention.

Ann's independent will is expressed, for example, when she refuses to put her hand in Korvo's, an intuitive gesture of resistance to Korvo's menacing appeals to her. Although she is under hypnosis at this time, her will is not only informed by insight but also expressed without the need for waking, rationalist evidence or support. *Whirlpool*, like other noir movies, and looking forward to Lynch's feminist (in)sight, which I'll discuss in Chapter 5, finds sympathy in a non-masculinist way of intuiting truth that puts conventional ways of knowing aside.

Thus Schickel's unexplained statement in his audio commentary that *Whirlpool* is not film noir (although he identifies the film as one of Preminger's "Fox Quintet"—*Laura* [1944], *Fallen Angel* [1945], *Whirlpool* [1949], *Where the Sidewalk Ends* [1950)], and *Angel Face* [1952]—all of which are centrally identified as original-cycle film noir) seems arbitrary, perhaps indebted to a lack of the pure "femme fatale" viewers often seek out in watching these films.

Ann Sutton does, of course, stand on the sidelines of the stereotypical "femme fatale," since she is beautiful, transgressive, and secretive. However, as I've tried to show, analysis of *Whirlpool* reveals much about postwar gender trauma in relation to women, despite Pauline Kael's dismissal of the film as "an atrocity" (15). While Bill does recover his trust in Ann in time for him to lead the police to discover the real murderer in Korvo, this ameliorative ending doesn't elide the movie's use of personality disorder to underscore the gender prisons in which women are locked up. Indeed the language of lockdown is invoked by Korvo, when he tells Ann (and she repeats later) that she is "locked away in a characterization of a serene and devoted wife."

Whirlpool posits a fairy tale ending in which Ann says to Bill, "I'll never lie to you." Bill responds, "You don't have to. I love you as you are," providing unconditional affirmation. This exchange underscores what has been at stake in the film: a lack of appreciation for female needs and desire and the tendency to project images onto women that reflect comfortably back on men and secure their psychological and social authority. The film's ending is quite interesting, because on the one hand, it reinscribes patriarchal authority, since Bill convinces the lieutenant to give Ann a chance and reimagine the crime as having not been committed by Ann. On the other hand, Bill manages somewhat inexplicably to move beyond "bellowing with wounded vanity." The film's recovery of "good" psychoanalysis supports Mary Ann Doane's reading of 1940s films about psychoanalysis subjecting women to a medical gaze that respecularizes women after they've been de-eroticized as a result of illness. Still, Doane's reading doesn't account for the extent to which some of these films, such as *Whirlpool*, foreground illness as a violent critique of patriarchy.

Doane suggests that 1940s films about female illness, such as *Possessed* and *Whirlpool* (she discusses the former at length and mentions the latter) "contain the most disruptive aspects of female spectatorship by specifying them as pathological" (226). The films may endorse the medical gaze and its enlightenment obsession with knowledge (Doane's comment that "light enables the look" certainly brings to mind the scene in *Laura* in which the investigative light is turned on Laura, as it is on Ann in *Whirlpool*). However, it is important to note that throughout most of *Whirlpool*, the medical gaze is shown to be flawed and at times unsympathetic and horrible. Louise's and Ann's pathologies are attempts to escape the social control the women are subjected to. While Doane is right that in many cases "the clinical is a most masculine eye," the language of the gaze repeats a methodology of contrasting masculine techniques of mastery (such as psychoanalysis) with female "unknowability," thus reinscribing the stereotypes surrounding female presence in film (the "realm of the unknowable is familiar to us in noir," says Doane [216]).

My own approach would be to reorient our response to female agency in film noir movies to explore these films' rupturing of specular systems of objectification to reimagine women in noir as they seek validation and forums for agency.[4] Bill Sutton's turnaround at the end of *Whirlpool* offers an interesting contrast with the notion with which I began this study and revisited in Chapter 2, Dev's brutal assertion in *Notorious* about Alicia that he should have known "that a woman like you could [never] change her spots." Such inflexibility in responding to the woman he supposedly loves—his insistence on "reading" her, rather than being with her—is a consequence of his overinvestment in a category, a set of ideas associated with the "femme fatale." The category trumps the woman herself and makes it impossible for the men to trust her, an idea that apparently interested Ben Hecht, who wrote both *Notorious* and *Whirlpool*. Think here, too, of Jake Gittes's cynical "reading" of Evelyn Mulwray: "Come on, Mrs. Mulwray—you've got your husband's girlfriend tied up in there."

In contrast, Bill, in the end, validates Ann, trusting her, saying to the Lieutenant, "a woman like Ann doesn't change suddenly. Some fingerprints and a few odd circumstances can't wipe out a woman's heart and character as if they never existed." While the comment reflects Bill's rekindled trust in Ann, the language interestingly echoes Devlin's dismissal of Alicia in *Notorious* when he fails to imagine that "a woman like you could ever change her spots."

To accept modern woman "as [she] is" would require not only the kind of imaginative sympathy the film calls for—"I want you to listen with an open mind," says Bill to the Lieutenant—but also acceptance of changed power relations, whereby men can share social space with a New Woman. *Whirlpool*, like *Leave Her to Heaven* and *Possessed*, portrays female desire as intense. The women in these films have passions and energy that aren't validated or acknowledged and are thus expressed covertly, unhealthily, or unlawfully. Mental disorders figure as effective, if desperate, avenues for escape and rebellion.

Part II Film Noir's Janus Face

4

Looking Back—*Victorinoir*: Modern Women and the Fatal(e) Progeny of Victorian Representations

As I've suggested throughout Part I, many film noir movies lend subjectivity to the independent women often referred to as "femmes fatales," depicting the psychological motives for becoming, or acting the role of, the "femme fatale." Contrary to popular culture's and film criticism's insistence that the deadly seductress figure defines American film noir, most noir movies suggest that women are forced into performing the role of "femme fatale" to escape social traps, thus offering a critique of the construction of the "femme fatale" on two levels. First, we see how women are forced to use their bodies and language to gain an upper hand in a society that habitually denies them freedom and culturally sanctioned opportunities. Second, many of these films expose the process by which the idea of the "femme fatale" is devised as a means of projecting male fear and anxiety onto the woman herself. The movies reflect how men in the culture project the idea of "femme fatale" as a label onto particular women in order to divide women into two easily regulated categories: "femmes fatales" and "angels in the house."

These latter categories are, of course, familiar to us from our knowledge of the representation of gender in Victorian literature and culture, and indeed, I want to argue that Victorian narrative provides important parallels for understanding these projections. Victorian novels struggling with issues of female power can usefully be seen as precursors to film noir, which inherits yet extends Victorian narrative's investigation of categorical representations of women as angel/whore, as "good girl"/ "femme fatale." Film noir's critique of binary representations of women, suggesting multiple portraits of strong, vulnerable women who resist simple categorization, is also anticipated in Victorian narrative.

Late-Victorian fiction and original cycle film noir register the crosscurrents, challenges, and anxieties of the modern period, and this historical link between Victorian narrative and Hollywood noir suggests some very interesting influences and continuities in representation. Certainly, to be culturally literate in modern America, one had to be familiar with British literature and culture. As Henry James, T. S. Eliot, and Raymond Chandler exemplify, modern American writers were often anglophiles, if not expatriates. To make the point from the perspective of American film history, Mark Glancy's book *When Hollywood Loved Britain* argues for the profound influence of Britain on American film of the 1930s and 1940s. While Glancy's focus is on issues of patriotism, the extensive list of films adapting Victorian novels (*The Mill on the Floss, David Copperfield, Great Expectations, Wuthering Heights, Jane Eyre, Dr. Jekyll and Mr. Hyde*, to name just a few) or featuring British talent (such as popular noir director Hitchcock, actors George Sanders and Laird Cregar, and noir screenwriter Joan Harrison) further demonstrates the important connections between Victorian culture and American film of the 1930s and 1940s.

More pointedly still, Guy Barefoot's book *Gaslight Melodrama: from Victorian London to 1940s Hollywood* repeatedly argues that Victorian London is a crucial source for film noir and 1940s Hollywood melodrama. While it's clear enough that "gaslight" noir films such as *Hangover Square, The Suspect*, and *The Spiral Staircase* invoke a nineteenth-century British context, Barefoot's analysis (along with Glancy's, Martha Vicinus's, Christine Gledhill's, and Helen Hanson's work drawing links between Victorian Gothic and 1940s melodrama) paves the way for understanding Victorian narrative as an important context for understanding film noir. Emphasizing connections between the Victorian gaslight city and the way Hollywood of the 1940s rehearsed this setting, Barefoot's book seeks to "investigate the often-conflicting attitudes evoked by the legacy of Victorianism and Victoriana traceable in Hollywood films, in films made in Britain, and in a wider cultural context" (12). Barefoot thus advances the possibility of pursuing these links with attention to gender, for which his focus on the evil lurking within the dark city has important implications.

My interest is in the extent to which Victorian narrative provides important parallels for understanding the representations of women and gender in film noir in the context of rapid cultural change and the advent of modernism. Engaged as it was with gender anxieties produced by changing social roles, Victorian fiction presented a ready model for early filmmakers. More specifically, representations of gendered time and space in late-Victorian novels offered, indeed, a "pre-history" for film noir: an avenue of investigation that noir films would be influenced by and would revisit repeatedly.

The "femme fatale" can be usefully redefined as sharing identity with the *femme moderne* who haunted nineteenth-century texts and then resurfaced as the "vamp" in silent film before the flourishing of film noir in the 1940s. These "fatal women" represent, on the one hand, the efforts of women to better position themselves and, on the other, the cultural opposition to formulations of modern female independence. My aim in introducing the Victorian period into a discussion of film noir is to broaden the cultural context from which film noir's "femme fatale" emerges in order to encourage finer readings of film noir movies and to expose the troubling reproduction and repetition of certain kinds of patterns in our ways of reading women, female agency, and narratives about powerful women.

The New Woman and "The Hidden Army" of World War II

Late nineteenth-century changes in gender roles were embraced and at the same time violently resisted. These shifts produced, in the late Victorian period, what Richardson and Willis call "the polyphonic nature of the debates around femininity at this time" that included public discourse that was at times "harmful and disparaging" (11, 13). Starting from the middle of the nineteenth century, there was, as Richardson and Willis recount, a dramatic increase of women in the work force; a gradual opening up of opportunities in education; a reevaluation and legislative reinvention of marriage, divorce, and property laws; and an increasing attention to the sexual double standard (see Richardson and Willis, 5–7). These substantive alterations in the lives and attitudes of women and men produced what Ella Hepworth Dixon called "amazing changes in the social life of women" (Ledger and Luckhurst, 86). While debates surrounding women's rights varied across issues such as sexuality, marriage, maternity, suffrage, and labor, the "New Women" agreed that a reinterpretation of women's social role was necessary for women to achieve greater independence and fulfillment:

> What the New Women did share was a rejection of the culturally defined feminine role and a desire for increased educational and career opportunities that would allow them to be economically self-sufficient.
>
> (Nelson, x)

Some New Women writers, such as M. Eastwood, were alert to the inflammatory language of empowerment invoked in popular commentary on the New Woman. In her 1894 essay "The New Woman in Fiction and in Fact," Eastwood hails the New Woman, as she parodies popular images of her, the "flashing, dashing, ripping, tripping creation, yclept the New Woman" (Ledger and Luckhurst, 90).

The New Woman was appropriated not only by feminist activists but also by men and women rejecting new conceptions of female independence. About suffrage, many middle-class women, such as Mary Ward, insisted on women's lack of "sound judgment" (Ledger and Luckhurst, 93) and decried, in 1889, the case for suffrage as a "total misconception of women's true dignity and special mission" (94). Boyd Winchester's article on "The Eternal Feminine," published in *Arena* in 1902, finds women's genius in their "sentiment," "imaginative sympathy," and "moral susceptibility," insisting that

> every one who cherishes the slightest regard for the rare virtues and qualities of sweet womanhood must resent and abhor the too manifest tendency of modern social, industrial, and educational innovations to unsex and abase our young women.
>
> (Nelson, 177)

Hyperbolic language in support and in defiance of the New Woman pervaded popular commentary. For Eastwood, the New Woman was "the weirdly bewitching, the soulful, the mysterious, the tricksy, the tragic, the electrifying, the intensely-intense, and utterly unfathomable new one" (90). Eastwood's participation in the invention of the legendary New Woman energized readers, while some commentary, like the critical attention later paid to the "electrifying" women in film noir, contributed to a sense of woman as "Other" and to increasingly bewildered responses to female social advancement.

A striking example of such negative mythifying is (the anti-New Woman) Ouida's reversal of conventional discussions of women of the period, an instance of backlash in 1894 that presages the postwar transposition of the independent woman into a "dangerous dame":

> The error of the New Woman (as of many an old one) lies in speaking of women as the victims of men, and entirely ignoring the frequency with which men are the victims of women. In nine cases out of ten the first to corrupt the youth is the woman. In nine cases out of ten also she becomes corrupt herself because she likes it.
>
> (Nelson, 157)

The passage suggests the extent to which the "bad women" become an effective vehicle for diverting energy for social change into forms of social hysteria, reflecting the generalized anxiety surrounding gender roles during times of transition. Susan Bordo notes, for example, that "the second half of the nineteenth century, concurrent with the first feminist wave . . . saw a virtual flood of artistic and literary images of the dark, dangerous, and evil female" (161). Bordo rightly observes that this is a recurring habit of representation "during periods when women are becoming independent and are asserting themselves politically and socially" (161).

The literature of the late-Victorian period certainly explored and tried to navigate these anxieties and contradictions, in part by constructing "angels in the house"[1] and by anticipating a continual resurgence of the "femme fatale" figure. Like many noir films, many nineteenth-century texts expose the "femme fatale" as a projection of male fears about the rise of independent women, the New Woman of both late Victorian England and postwar America. As Bram Dijkstra has said about the turn-of-the-century "femme fatale" figure as she is represented in art of the period,

> [l]iving under clouds and surf that seem like steam rising from the boiling cauldron of the elemental sea, these women represent that unabashed independence and elemental sense of freedom that men of 1900 feared, and found most fascinating, in the viragoes of their day. In the very directness of their passion and strength, these women embodied the paradox of the self-possessed and therefore hated, yet so very delectable and admirable New Woman, she who had thrown off the trappings of the household nun and had toppled her weak and fainting mother's pedestal.
>
> (265)

The repetition of "elemental" in the passage correctly identifies the force of ideation surrounding the female threat to established norms and conventions. Indeed, Rebecca Stott has observed that the presence of the "femme fatale" figure in late Victorian culture and literature "takes her place amongst degeneration anxieties, the rise of invasion scares, anxieties about 'sexuality' and 'race,' and concerns about cultural 'virility' and fitness" (22), just as, I would add, film noir explores anxieties about changed social and sexual roles of women in post-World War II America. As Stott claims, "the constitution of the *femme-fatale*-as-sign depends upon *what* else (besides Woman) is considered to be culturally invasive or culturally and politically Other at any historical point" (44).

For the women who had experienced independence and new forms of self-sufficiency in wartime America, the alienation caused by postwar changes in attitude was palpable. Film noir's sociocultural setting is one characterized by extreme gender anxiety, as men coming home from the war wondered what their wives had been doing when they were away and as women were driven back into the domestic sphere to resume functions as wives and mothers after a period of independence and new experiences as part of the work force during the war. When women entered the workforce—18 million women, six million for the first time—they discovered a venue for female desire, ambition, and for enhanced recognition of the contributions women could make to society and in the marketplace. According to Frank, joining the work force "markedly affected women's personal sense of themselves" (Frank et al., 17). Frank, Ziebarth, and Field recount myriad stories of the women who took pride in their contributions to the war effort, as well as their new and increased salaries. Lola Weixel comments, for example, on the changed perceptions of women welders:

> We were going to get in on the ground floor and be welders for ever and ever. It was almost an art, as well as a skill. It was a very beautiful kind of work. At the end of the day I always felt I had accomplished something. There was a product. There was something to be seen.
>
> (qtd. in Frank et al., 17)

While these women had experienced a dramatic movement from the margins to the center of social production, after the war, many of these women were fired or laid off: "As dramatically as they had come into the war plants," Deslippe explains, "they left or, in most cases, were fired":

> By the spring [of 1945], over 300,000 women had been laid off; that figure climbed to over 3,000,000 by the next year. In Detroit, the proportion of women in the automobile industry work force fell to 7.5 percent from 25 percent; in Los Angeles only 14 percent of the women who had worked in aircraft plants during the war still held their jobs in mid-1946. Nationally, women's share of employment in durable goods industries plummeted 50 percent. Many of these workers had considerable difficulty securing new jobs. A survey of 20,000 women workers in Detroit revealed that 72 percent of them had not yet found new jobs weeks after being released, despite their efforts. A note of desperation marked their search for work. "I was looking around madly for something to do because I didn't have that much money to last very long," one divorced woman with children reported. Those fortunate to secure employment took severe pay

cuts: women who had earned an average of 85 to 90 cents an hour were now accepting jobs that paid only 45 to 50 cents an hour.

(Deslippe, 13)

Government and industry began its dismantling of "the hidden army," one wartime government film's designation for wartime female employment (Frank et al., 19). One riveter, Edna Artman, recalls,

[w]hen the war was over, they tried their darndest to get rid of the women. They said women were unstable, that we'd been absent too much, that we had our kids to look after. In my case they said I was too fat! Ford went from 18,000 to 2,000 women after they'd hired back in '46.

(Frank et al., 20)

In her *Feminist Lives in Victorian England,* Philippa Levine devotes a chapter to the subject of women "Invading the Public Sphere" (126), as they discovered self-sufficiency and new venues for female agency in the second half of the nineteenth century. So, too, American women in the 1940s marched into the public sphere, having new social roles to play. This produced a cultural discourse and popular representations characterized both by meaningful change and by backlash.

Literature, film, and gender invasion

Victorian narrative and film noir—both products of modern culture—are thus not only mutually informing, but also indicative of the continual problems we have in representing and in analyzing and understanding the complex experience of women in the social world. Like the cultural preoccupation with the "femme fatale" figure in film noir, the New Woman functioned as both a symbol of female power and an opportunity for dominant cultural voices to categorize and subordinate threatening calls for female agency. As Richardson and Willis note,

the late nineteenth-century media reduction of the New Women to stereotypes might be considered a strategy of control, aimed at containing the threat they posed to the status quo. The bicycling Amazon and ugly bluestocking of caricature are more immediately accessible and memorable figures than women concerned with social political change and thus were often used as a way of obscuring the latter's goals.

(28)

In 1887, Rider Haggard warned of female incursions in his immensely popular novel *She*, an adventure tale about a male journey to the African Kor, where the dominant, powerful, and immortal Ayesha, "She Who Must Be Obeyed," resides and rules the Amahaggar people. We know from early in the novel that "women among the Amahaggar live upon conditions of perfect equality with the men, and are not held to them by any binding ties" (63). As its preoccupation with female power suggests, the novel was, according to Elaine Showalter, a "complicated response to female literary dominance, as well as to British imperialism and fears of manly decline in the face of female power" (83). Showalter links the Amahaggar women directly to late nineteenth-century New Women: "Like the New Women novelists, they have renounced their dependencies on men" (85). Further suggesting the topical concerns about female social advancement, Showalter observes that it is no coincidence that the novel's main narrator, Holly, is a Cambridge don, since "the year when [Holly's and Leo's] quest begins, 1881, is also the year women were first admitted to the Cambridge examinations, and when, symbolically, the strongholds of male knowledge begin to fall" (85). The novel registers contemporary questions surrounding female independence and social advancement, questions that included a baffled wondering about the fate of (or "fatal" end to) male control over social institutions.

If *She* articulates anxiety about gender invasion and inversion ("Evidently the terrible *She* had determined to go to England, and it made me shudder to think what would be the result of her arrival there" [192–3]), parallel backlash concerns were echoed in 1945 in a *New York Times* story about women's growing influence in Hollywood. The article, "Hollywood Bows to the Ladies," offers the following: "Picture-making, like everything else, is coming more and more under feminine influence. The ladies, no longer content with being just glamorous, are invading in increasing numbers the production field, a sphere hitherto almost entirely masculine" (qtd. in Biesen, 127). The invasion language, as in *She*, registers the threat of female autonomy, independence, and passage into social spheres of influence: "This woman," says Holly, *She*'s narrator, "had confounded and almost destroyed my moral sense, as indeed she must confound all who looked upon her superhuman loveliness" (173). This "[confounding]" and admixture is echoed in the vampiric language invoked in publicity materials for *The Postman Always Rings Twice* (1946). About Lana Turner's Cora Smith, MGM declared, "Her name is Cora . . . . *She Gets Into Men's Blood . . . And Stays There!*" (qtd. in Biesen, 123).

Like *She* (as well as *Dracula*, which I'll discuss later), many film noir movies reveal, and yet also critique, destructive fantasies about female power that elide complex female identity. In most film noir movies, however, despite cultural preoccupations with the "femme fatale" figure, sympathy for the independence and struggles of women emerges. It is thus of great interest that these women's stories are then suppressed by critics, who reduce represented complex female experience to the simple role of the "femme fatale"—a role that then is codified and solidified as a defining feature of film noir.

Something similar is forewarned in readings of nineteenth-century fiction—in, for example, the reception of "cold" Estella, "frigid" Sue Bridehead, or most tellingly, readings of *Tess of the D'Urbervilles*. While some critics of Thomas Hardy's 1891 novel judge Tess's seductiveness (i.e., "she asked for it"), Rebecca Stott has rightly observed the strangeness of this pattern in Hardy criticism "which often assumes a male audience who know about the wiles of women" [172]). Similarly, Ann Ardis argues that by devaluing New Women fiction, late-Victorian male critics "produced a male image of culture and history" (57). Psychosocial assumptions and desires have, in these cases, resulted in canonized readings of film and literature that marginalize the stories of women and gender that are so central to nineteenth and twentieth-century narrative. Such projections of gender characteristics, like the contemporary (recent) male critical responses to film noir, as discussed in Chapter 2, should be noted as points on a historical continuum on which gender categories are continually reasserted. My concern is that because we are so preoccupied with the category of the "femme fatale," we are blind to the stories of the women in film noir and to the varied historical backdrops that inform these stories.

Divided realms

The representation of women in noir, as in Victorian literature, seems powerfully linked to divisions of space and time, a compartmentalization of experience that is, I would argue, critiqued by the logic of the texts in which the phenomenon appears. The drive to rigidly oppose realms—notably public versus private worlds; past versus present; city versus country—is expressed in Victorian fiction and in film noir at the same time as these spaces are identified in terms of gender. These oppositions, and our responses to them, have profound consequences for the cultural mediation of gender roles, in representation and in society, since these categories mold experience (as Foucault has taught us) into sharply regulated and often deeply oppressive spheres of influence. Indeed, I would argue along with Rebecca Stott that the "femme fatale" is a deeply Foucauldian concept: "In Foucauldian terms what we are witnessing is a process engaged not in stamping out the illicit and the anomalous but producing and regulating it" (25). I would add to Stott's commentary on late Victorian imbrications of the "femme fatale" that the construct, unleashed and expressed in order to be institutionalized, is alive and well in contemporary culture. The "femme fatale" is a product of dualistic thinking about women, but I hope that my discussion of the recurrence of these patterns helps to support my larger claim that there is a kind of urgency in the need to continue to put pressure on this category. The persistent projection onto women of mutually exclusive categories of being in the world often has tragic implications for women who stray from their roles or want to break down the oppositions that bind them.

Victorian narrative provides an important source for film noir in its preoccupation with the public and private dualism. Nineteenth-century literature very familiarly rehearses a dichotomy between the corrupt public realm and sacred domesticity. For example, in *Great Expectations*, Dickens calls Wemmick's home his private "Castle" world, and each day when he walks to work at "Little Britain," his face literally changes: "Wemmick got dryer and harder as we went along, and his mouth tightened into a post-office" (232). Wemmick becomes literally schizophrenic. In the following passage, Jaggers discovers that Wemmick has a meaningful private domestic life, which collides with the office world of Little Britain:

> "What's all this?" said Mr. Jaggers. "You with an old father, and you with pleasant and playful ways?"
> "Well!" returned Wemmick. "If I don't bring 'em here, what does it matter?"
> [Later, Jaggers repeats,] "You with a pleasant home?"
>
> (424)

Here Dickens gestures toward a critique of the compartmentalizing of experience, a division of space that enforces repression and impedes human contact, as Wemmick's transformation on the walk to work exemplifies. While Dickens's treatment of Wemmick's double life is treated comically, it also constitutes a kind of *Victorinoir*, a representation of ostensibly efficient social systems ready to break down or explode if provoked. *Victorinoir* threatens social stability. In this case, Wemmick's domestic castle and Aged P., seemingly protected by an artificial moat from the corrupting influences of London, are less a safe haven than a sign of impending rupture; as Pip observes after the revelation, "I had never seen [Wemmick and Jaggers] on such ill terms; for generally they got on very well indeed together" (426). Pip's commentary on this scene reveals the implications of failing to keep public and private worlds separate, itself indicative of the fragility of the boundaries that divide these realms.

Male ideation and women fighting back

Film noir not only rehearses these dichotomies but shows the dangers of crossing from one side of an opposition to the other. Because these boundaries that structure the noir and Victorian worlds are gendered, when women cross these lines, they become a threat to dominant male culture, as Rita Hayworth's Gilda does when she vamps for male audiences at the same time as she elicits sympathy for becoming increasingly victimized by Ballen's and Johnny's tyranny.

Gilda provides a good example of the problem with generalizing about representations of women in film noir. In 1956, Jacques Siclier wrote about "the relentless misogyny" in film noir, noting about Rita Hayworth that her role was to "Be beautiful and keep silent . . . she has nothing to say" (Palmer, 70). In fact, Hayworth's "crime" in *Gilda* may be that she speaks up. Gilda reveals that what's fatal in the "femme fatale" is the persistent ideation surrounding women. She calls attention to the victimization of women: first, through her several performances of "Put the Blame on Mame" (one, plaintively; one, humming; one, aggressively, as a part of her striptease); second, through her use of language as a weapon. Gilda in fact silences Johnny when she implicitly refers to the sexual meaning of "dancing," and disarms Johnny when she feminizes him by repeatedly referring to him as "pretty." Gilda's wit and her performances constitute a rebellion against Ballen's and Johnny's narrow construction of her identity, a misogynist representation of women within the film that is not—as a result of Gilda's power, intelligence, and invitation to sympathize with her—endorsed by the film.

The New Woman mounted a similar rebellion, a point Ann Ardis makes in connection to New Women fiction: "In some of these novels the convention of omniscience is also dismantled by female characters who assert their autonomy from a male narrator—thereby turning what Mikhail Bakhtin terms the 'monologic' structuring of realistic narrative into a polyphonic form" (3). Ardis's insight is analogous to Karen Hollinger's discussion of *Gilda* that I referred to in Chapter 2. For Hollinger, *Gilda* demonstrates female resistance to male-controlled narrative in the form of voice-over. Gilda's striptease "[dismantles]" Johnny's hold on her, at the same time as it expresses her frustration and anger.

Gilda's charismatic performances, like her wit, disrupt male voice-over, narration, and control, substituting female autonomy for male ideation. One thinks here of Simone de Beauvoir's comments about Brigitte Bardot, that "her eroticism is not magical, but aggressive": "But the male feels uncomfortable, if, instead of a doll of flesh and blood, he holds in his arms a conscious being who is sizing him up" (115). This is a useful gloss on Gilda's deflation of Johnny, her "sizing up" of him, at one point suggesting to him that "[a]ny psychiatrist would tell you that your thought associations are very revealing."

Rita Hayworth's famed "Put the Blame on Mame" number contributed to Rita Hayworth's status as pin-up, which, according to Maria Elena Buszek, reflected female agency in important ways. At the end of her chapter "New Frontiers: Sex, Women, and World War II," Buszek says,

> [t]he pin-up provided an outlet through which women might assert that their unconventional sexuality could coexist with conventional ideals of professionalism, patriotism, decency, and desireability—in other words suggesting that a woman's sexuality could be expressed as part of her whole being.
>
> (231)

Buszek's use of the term "decency" is interesting, given Gilda's first lines in *Gilda*, which play on a double meaning of "decent." Ballen calls to Gilda's bedroom, "Gilda, are you decent?" to which she replies, "Me? Sure, I'm decent." This is another instance of Gilda's manipulation of language, the gendered jockeying over the word "decent" reflecting female self-awareness and power to control discourse and meaning. In the context of the pin-up, as explored by Buszek, it is easy to see how the role of Gilda quickly was reduced to the "femme fatale." About the most popular pin-up, the famed "Varga Girl," Buszek says:

> The Varga Girl's strange ideal clarifies how, like the government-shaped ideal of home-front womanhood, this World War II pin-up was an ambitious composite of contradictory feminine ideals that, once embodied, presented a new and monstrous beauty.
>
> (186)

Rita Hayworth's image, like the other pin-ups who were "neither domestic nor submissive" (Buszek, 186), would eclipse Hayworth's life and properly nuanced readings of Gilda, as a result of cultural obsessions with the "femme fatale" figure.

The Victorian era had its own Gildas. If there were no pin-ups per se, there were strong female characters in Victorian fiction who rebelled against male control and stereotypes of female submissiveness. Authors like Dickens, the Brontes, Thomas Hardy, George Eliot, and Henry James forced a mediation between extreme conceptions of gender, whereby rebellions are repressed, and compromises are, in the end, achieved. As the "tamed" Estella, Jane and Rochester (in *Jane Eyre*), Cathy Linton and Hareton (in *Wuthering Heights*), Bathsheba (*Far from the Madding Crowd*), Dorothea (in *Middlemarch*), and Isabel Archer (*The Portrait of a Lady*) exemplify, the extent to which a character compromises with an opposing force (the city, sexuality, the class system, and society in general) measures his/her success as a character.[2] In noir, we see the same issues, the same relegation of women to the "natural" domestic realm, the eternal realm, but these dichotomies are troubled in such a way as to call attention to the ideological contradictions in dominant culture—to the fact, for example, that it's not so easy to keep women from contesting their oppressively circumscribed social roles.

In film noir, male violence against women often highlights this difficulty. The more powerful women are imagined to be, often, the more violent is the male reply. In Nicholas Ray's *In a Lonely Place* (1950), Dix Steele's temper (as embodied in his name) reflects anxiety about the loss of control over changing conceptions of gender, a force of the narrative submerged in the story of a romantic idealist whose desire to control is upset. A common noir trope, the woman (here, Laurel Gray) is the signal of male loss of mastery, as the couple fall in love while Laurel becomes increasingly concerned about Dix's controlling demeanor and violent temper. Details and scenes in the film additionally reflect repressed sex and gender troubles: Laurel's relationship with massage therapist Martha ("she beats me black and blue"); Mel's dysfunctional devotion to Dix, featured as "feminine" submissiveness; and the suggestion that screenwriter Dix sublimates his violent tendencies into Hollywood scripts about murder.

One scene in particular highlights the film's interest in gender inversions. Dix Steele (played by Humphrey Bogart) is placed in a female realm, the kitchen, and bends a grapefruit knife back into shape, since he is ignorant of its proper use. As Laurel's concerns about Dix's violent temper mount in the film, this moment suggests the crossing of gender boundaries and evokes a threat of violence, the latter point well articulated by Dana Polan, who says that "*In a Lonely Place* shows a violence installed within the heart of the dominant culture, ready to break out at any moment" (46).

I discussed the homme fatale in my last chapter, but I do want to reemphasize throughout this project the difficulty we have as readers and viewers in wresting control of the narrative from the psychotic men that people film noir. Close reading of many film noir movies shows such men struggling with the failure of their ideals concerning women to obtain in the actual world.

Male passivity

Juxtaposed to these violent figures are the passive and powerless males, who similarly reflect anxiety about female independence and rebellion. Such is the case for Thomas Hardy's male protagonist Jocelyn Pierston, whose name inverts the masculine threat of a character like "Dix Steele." Pierston appears in Thomas Hardy's last-published novel, *The Well-Beloved*, published in 1897, though written five years earlier. In his search for "the well-beloved," evanescent images of male notions of female perfection articulated in schematic narrative terms, Pierston feels helpless in his attempts to escape the cycle of idealization and disillusionment; the empowerment of woman as image clashes with the image's incapacity to obtain persistent gratification for male observers. This process of ideation is forewarned in the concern of Holly in Haggard's novel that once She has died, "elsewhere we may find her, and, as I believe, shall find her, but not here." The idea of (and the incipience of) the desired but inaccessible woman permeates the atmosphere, reflecting cultural ambivalence about the enticing independent woman and anxiety about male power to control her.

The pattern also repeats itself throughout film noir, exemplified in Scotty's obsessive ideation surrounding Madeleine in *Vertigo* (1958), or even Jeff Markham's initial vision of Kathy Moffett in *Out of the Past* (1947), which inevitably gives way to his own abandonment of agency ("Baby I don't care") and then disillusionment when she ceases to serve his ideal. At that point, like many male protagonists in late-Victorian literature and film noir, Markham becomes wholly passive to his fate. As Hardy's Pierston says about the "Well-Beloved," "I grew so accustomed to these exits and entrances that I resigned myself to them quite passively" (39). In *She*, Holly is also rendered passive with regard to female power: "We could no more have left her [She] than a moth can leave the light that destroys it" (182). In late-Victorian narrative and in film noir, the failure to come to terms with female agency is reflected in a pattern of representation in which male protagonists are unwilling to take responsibility for trauma and disruption. While these texts seem preoccupied with male impotence and passivity, such attention to men's helplessness masks the scapegoating of female desire and ambition as fatal.

Repression and out-ing the past

Gender trauma, as I've been arguing, strongly links film noir and Victorian narrative, which are both modernist reflections of disruptions of sex and gender roles. Often these disruptions are figured as hidden; often as violent eruptions. Dana Polan's reading of *In a Lonely Place*, for example, touches on the closeness of such violence to the surface of things, the proximity of criminality to "normal" domesticity (as is figured in the bent-back grapefruit knife) and conventional divisions of space and time. This latter organization of experience, dividing past from present, becomes a major source of anxiety for characters in Victorian fiction and film noir. Further, the anguished relation to the past is often figured in terms of deep unease about sex and gender. The heroes of *Out of the Past*, *In a Lonely Place*, and *The Blue Dahlia*, like so many noir protagonists, ambivalently repress the past, in effect "criminalizing" the troubled Victorian longing to achieve a continuity between past and present. As Maggie Tulliver says in *The Mill on the Floss*, "If the past is not to bind us, where can duty lie? We should have no law but the inclination of the moment" (475).

The endings of some noir films are deceiving in this respect. *Gilda*, *Johnny Guitar*, and *The Big Heat* end happily on the surface—Johnny and Gilda reunite, as do Johnny Guitar and Vienna, and Dave Bannion has reclaimed his position as detective-hero. But the violence and despair associated with the past throughout these films suggests that the violence and retribution will continue, a notion echoed by Colin McArthur at the end of his reading of *The Big Heat*. Although Bannion is back on the job, his earlier domestic life has been demolished. The poster in his office—"Give blood—now!"—ironically comments on the jaded heroism of the work of police detectives: "the bleak cycle has begun once more" (78). In *Gilda*, we see a rebellion against the Victorian straining to resolve the breaks between the past and the present. As Johnny Farrell viscerally and contemptuously dismisses Gilda's overtures to discuss their former relationship, the film shows how ineffectual Johnny's attempt is to repress the past and to suppress Gilda, whose intelligence and wit, as well as her sexuality and anger, frustrate him in scene after scene.

In film noir there is very often a tension between a central lesson of the movie, which is that the past must be revisited or redressed, and the fatalistic insistence on the part of the male protagonist that he repress or escape from the past, a past that is usually characterized by his having been entrapped by sexuality (via the "femme fatale") and/or violence (fighting criminals, engaging in criminal activity, or soldiering in a war). The past thus functions as a fatal other, allied with the threat of the woman.

In *Out of the Past*, Jeff Markham/Bailey must inevitably renounce his dream of running his gas station and marrying his angelic and passive country girlfriend Ann in the sleepy town of Bridgeport, California. In an inevitable return of the repressed, his past relations with the "femme fatale" Kathie Moffett (Jane Greer) and the corrupt Whit Sterling (Kirk Douglas) resurface; Jeff's repressed past life as a cynical private investigator who fell in love with a deadly seductress proves, in the end, fatal. Although the woman is identified within the film and in critical discourse as the single source of desolation in the film, it is the male protagonist's failure of vision, his failure to interpret experience, that dooms him in *Out of the Past*. Kathy Moffett herself points this out (as quoted in Chapter 1) when she says to Jeff, "I never pretended to be anything but what I was. You just didn't see it. That's why I left you."[3] In its associations between the dangerous woman and the past, film noir recalls representations of "She" and of Dracula and the female vampires that attend Dracula, as atavistic regressive forces threatening to pull stalwart men back in time, back to a different social order of things.

One thinks, for example, of Lucy Westenra in Stoker's *Dracula*, who becomes a "femme fatale" because of her desires, desires that violate sexual and social taboos. Carol A. Senf comments that Bram Stoker was "so horrified at sexual openness that he chooses the female vampire as a shocking metaphor of the new liberated woman" (64).[4] Stott notes that "it is perhaps no coincidence that 1897, the year of the publication of *Dracula*, saw the amalgamation of the different suffrage societies into the National Union of Women's Suffrage Societies" (73). And indeed *Dracula* plays out its conservatism by insisting on maintaining all of the cultural oppositions it represents: public/private, city/country, past/present. In addition to showing a violation of space (Dracula, the sexual Eastern other, invades the space of stalwart Western domestic stability), the novel makes possible a critique of the arbitrary division of past and present. Further, in its tortured presentation of the demarcation of cultural spaces, Victorian anxiety about changing gender roles frames an important narrative model for film noir.

In his fascinating essay about the haunting of Victorian conceptions of character in the modern period, Ronald R. Thomas sees Dracula not as a figure of the past but a force of the future. For Thomas, Dracula's role as a modern force of transformation is often expressed in the cinematic effects associated with adaptations of Stoker's novel. Dracula is a "spectre" of the fantastic technologies of incipient modernism.

Thomas argues that the novel takes on "the real" in ways that make the prestidigitation of film a perfect medium for superseding "the two principal orthodoxies of the nineteenth-century novel: the myth of historical progress and the fantasy of the authentic self" (305). Stoker's novel came "on the scene" around the same time as did cinema, Lumiere's cinematographic wonders premiering in 1895, two years before *Dracula* was published. Dracula is, thus, like the New Woman, and, indeed, like cinema, a shape-shifting force whose powers threaten the status quo (the perceived "real").

> Dracula is more an agent of the liberating, subversive powers of modernity than he is of the power of the past. Those older forces, and the ideologies of the self they embodied, were more properly represented by the Victorian century that was reeling into the past as the novel was being published and the cinema was being born.
>
> (Thomas, 307)

The perspective Thomas brings to bear is important not only because it reinforces the significance of Victorian culture and ideology to modern representation—"'the movies,'" says Thomas, "have become the principal medium through which the Victorian novel, and even Victorian culture, has maintained its ghostly afterlife in modern society" (289)—but also because it underscores the interplay between threatening new forces and the backlash conservatism that these new powers give rise to. Thomas explains the nostalgia initiated by late-nineteenth-century transformations as "phantom shadows of the Victorian characters we can no longer be" (306).

The seductions of Dracula thus figure paradoxically as the prestidigitations of a new and modern world and as a forced eruption of the past that is itself alternately a safe sociocultural haven and a nest of uncivilized histories. In this way, Dracula does the cultural work of the so-called femme fatale, evoking a frightening future and a seemingly innocent but secretly guilty past.

Film noir conjures up the independent and imminent New Woman, and the Victorian novel haunts film noir like the undead. The visitation of the past resonates profoundly in film noir's representation of repressed histories, whether such failed forgetting is about violence experienced during the war; male friendships forged during the war lost to postwar resumption of conventional sexual and social roles; Johnny's and Gilda's unrevealed failed romance from the past; or various other traumas or formative histories reverberating, often obliquely, in the lives of male and female characters in noir.

The horror novels of the Victorian period in particular look forward to film noir. These novels problematize the Victorian inheritance of romantic confidence that a meaningful link can be established between the past and the present. They call into question this romantic assumption about the forward progress of history. Stoker's *Dracula*, for example, is about the sexualized savage beast wreaking havoc on western civilization. Similarly, *Dr. Jekyll and Mr. Hyde* and *The Picture of Dorian Gray* are explicitly about the violent consequences of repressing the past, whether in the form of (uncivilized) bestial sexuality in Stoker and Stevenson or in the form of the aging process (immortal youth repressing mortality) in Wilde's novel. If, as in mainstream Victorian fiction, the continuities between past and present are manageable, Victorian culture values making the connection between past and present, since the past provides a meaningful context in which to understand the present. In Victorian horror, however, we see the limits of Victorian faith in the ability to forge these links. This doubt becomes the *Victorinoir* underbelly of nineteenth-century fiction.

On the one hand, in *Dracula*'s bizarre postscript, Stoker gestures toward resolution through repression. At the novel's conclusion, years after the men and Mina destroy Dracula, when Jonathan and Mina go to Transylvania, we are told that "[e]very trace of all that had been was blotted out" (382). On the other hand, the final enforcement of Victorian repression of the dark side does little to ameliorate the story's emphasis on the violent consequences of compartmentalizing "the Other"—all that Dracula represents (sexuality, the East, and an uncivilized past) and the inevitable failure of this repression.

Interestingly, the exhortation to repress, to "blot out" past suffering, is, in one noir film, explicitly made from father John Forbes to his son Tommy in Andre de Toth's *Pitfall* (1948): Tommy asks, "Daddy, what makes a dream?" Forbes answers, "The mind is like a very wonderful camera . . . evidently, from the day we're born, the mind takes pictures and stores them away. Now and then one of those pictures comes loose in our sleep and that becomes a dream; so the trick is, take only good pictures and have only good dreams." At one level, in psychological terms, repression and projection surely drive this narrative. The Forbes family insists on restoring a repressed middle-class existence after John Forbes has an affair with Mona and kills Smiley, all of which redounds on Mona. However, there are severe social inequities (and iniquities) resulting from gender and class that are represented in *Pitfall*: Mona is the voice of critical commentary in the film (much like Gloria Grahame's Debby Marsh in *The Big Heat*, another misunderstood and ill-treated non-domestic woman in noir). She gets, as Eddie Muller says,

> the rawest deal. She's arrested for the murder of MacDonald. And the last Forbes sees of her, she's being swallowed into the maw of the injustice system. He can't even muster a "Tough luck, kid." . . . While John Forbes stewed over his indiscretion, Mona Stevens had to cope with the fixation of a horny married man, the return of a vengeful ex-con, and the obsessions of a psychotic stalker.
>
> (*Dark City*, 95)

This film, which presents a sympathetic non-domestic woman and shows her being scapegoated, bears some resemblance to Lucy Westenra's non-domesticity. "Why can't they let a girl marry three men?" Lucy asks; unsurprisingly, she is cursed and her sexuality transposed into evil (68). With a "voluptuous" and "wanton" smile, Lucy casts "a spell" on Arthur, who kills the "femme fatale" "like a figure of Thor" to restore the idea of pure Lucy that had come under attack (222).[5] Like *Dracula*, film noir movies represent cultural fears concerning the loss of old sources of power and fear of the new sources of power: "Women," says Bram Dijkstra, "who wanted to usurp part of man's place [in creation] were going against nature, becoming mock-men themselves, caricatures of masculinity, viragoes" (211).

Film noir reworks the *Victorinoir* cultural logic that seeks alternately to express and contain these anxieties by representing desperate women facing the challenges of modern existence. While film noir's tone is often defined in terms of male despair and entrapment (evoked poetically by Jeff Bailey's "I'm caught in a frame and all I can see is the frame" in *Out of the Past*, or Brad's "I'm backed up in a dark corner and I don't know who's hitting me" in *The Dark Corner* [1946]), these films also articulate the traps laid for women. One recalls Susan's evocative line in *The Big Combo* (1955): "I live in a maze, Mr. Diamond, a strange blind and blackened maze and all of the twisting paths lead back to Mr. Brown." The evocation here, however, bespeaks the helplessness of desiring modern women confined by social rules enforced by men that govern female activity. Far more often than is acknowledged, these women aren't evil "femmes fatales" but are *femmes modernes*, only interpreted as "femmes fatales" diagetically by unreliable male characters, then by viewers and critics unable to resist the seductiveness of reading women as wicked. The coding of these women as "femmes fatales" casts female assertion of authority as "fatal"; female agency is then appropriated by male protagonists who are themselves deeply violent (hommes fatales). There is, for example, Humphrey Bogart's Dix Steele, as discussed above, or many of Robert Ryan's men. These men act violently to restore conventional power relations, exemplifying transmutations of the patterns in *Victorinoir*.

Victorinoir expresses repressed cultural rage at female rebellion. This is best illustrated in the persecution of female vampires: the killing of Lucy in *Dracula*; the men's execution of Carmilla in Le Fanu's story.[6] Female vampire energy, symbolic of women going against social norms, is appropriated by male culture, mythified anew, "[figures] of Thor" acting violently to restore the "proper" power differential in the regulation of sex and gender identities.

The extremity of repression and projection displayed in movies like *Pitfall* speaks to persistent obsessions with maintaining clearly demarcated cultural spaces, a way of representing experience which Victorian narrative and film noir reproduce at the same time as their stories reveal the destructiveness of the effort. The destabilization of social orders certainly generates much of the drive in Victorian horror, which anticipates, as I've suggested above, film noir's concern with repression and its ultimate portrayal of the return of the repressed. This failure of repression, according to film noir and Victorian horror texts like *Dracula*, *Dr. Jekyll and Mr. Hyde*, and *The Picture of Dorian Gray*, thus manifests itself as Victorian energy turned to hate. The violence that had, in short, represented the underbelly of the system in Victorian culture becomes the dominant mode in modern culture and film noir.

The city

The dangers of imagining experience in terms of strict opposition and the failure to resolve these dichotomies are also played out in film noir's interest in the motif of city versus country (or "the natural" world), a rearticulated version of the battle between the domestic angel and non-domestic woman. Again, the noir fictional world recalls, on the surface, Victorian representations of the city as tainted and corrupt. For example, Pip's arrival at Barnard's Inn in London constitutes the first in a series of disappointments to his great expectations: "I thought it had the most dismal trees in it, and the most dismal sparrows, and the most dismal cats, and the most dismal houses (in number half a dozen or so), that I had ever seen" (196). In noir, the city's role is paradoxically antagonistic and an expression of the characters' own inner conflicts: as paranoid nightmare, for example, in Jules Dassin's *Night and the City*, reflecting HUAC witch hunts taking place in America in the late 1940s and early 1950s.

Years later, as film noir flourishes in the 1970s, in the neo-noir *Klute* (1971), Donald Sutherland plays John Klute, whose origins and residence in the Pennsylvania suburbs highlight Bree Daniel's excessively urban lifestyle as a psychologically conflicted call girl (Figure 4.1). She says to him, "Did we get you a little, Klute, the sin and glitter of the big city?" He replies, "Oh that's so pathetic."

This kind of pitting of city against country, where the "femme fatale" resides unnaturally in an urban den of iniquity, is emphatically portrayed in John Dahl's *The Last Seduction* (1994), in which Manhattan's Bridget Gregory stands so counter to the small town of Beston, New York (where she's on the lam) that she hides in her car to avoid the relentless assault of "Good Morning!"s from Beston's cheerful inhabitants. Bridget puts out a cigarette in a cake she finds in Mike's refrigerator that has written on it "Love, Grandma." She is so clearly an emanation of the dark, cynical city that she takes as a pseudonym "Wendy Kroy," a version of "New York" spelled backward. As Judith Walkowitz has said about women entering the public world in late nineteenth-century London,

Figure 4.1   Bree Daniels (Jane Fonda) and the city in *Klute* (1971). BFI; *Klute* © Warner Bros. Inc. and Gus Productions, Inc. All Rights Reserved.

the city, for the New Woman of the late Victorian period and, I would add, film noir existed as both "a place of danger and of possibility" for women (80). The fascination of these female portraits emerges out of the agonistic relationship between the *femme moderne* and her environment, a struggle between women's desires and ambitions and the psychosocial traumas and conquests that follow such determination.

Case study: Bleak House (1852; 1920)

The *Victorinoir* link between a dangerous past, a tainted city, and the *femme moderne* can be seen in Maurice Elvey's fascinating silent film adaptation of Dickens's *Bleak House* (which first appeared in series installments in 1852). Elvey's 1920 film, written for the screen by William J. Elliot, looks back to the high Victorian critique of social hypocrisy, class oppression, the violently brutal conditions of the poor in the city, but does so through the lens of a noir style and point of view, emphasizing death and the failure of social institutions to address human need and desire.

This adaptation of *Bleak House* interestingly isolates and focuses on the story of Lady Dedlock, the mysterious and suspicious dark lady of the novel. Contemporary reviewers of the film were surprised, as the following comment by *The Bioscope* suggests, by Elvey's and Elliot's choice to foreground the story of Lady Dedlock:

> Though one reads "Bleak House" to renew acquaintance with such delightful people as Mr. Turveydrop and Mr. Chadband, Mr. Skimpole, and Mrs. Jellyby, Cadby or Grandfather Smallweed, and cares very little about Lady Dedlock's early love affair or Mr. Tulkinghorne's investigations, there is no doubt whatever that the investigations which lead up to the murder of the solicitor are sufficient to form the basis of an excellent film drama.
>
> (February 26, 1920)

The review observes, as the comment suggests, the story's emphasis on the anonymity, distress, and alienation of outsider figures in the social world. Indeed, the film focuses on the victims of modern social institutions, Lady Dedlock, Captain Hawdon (existentially renamed "Nemo" in the novel, Latin for "Nobody"), and the desperate and doomed young street urchin Jo. Lady Dedlock is the central of these *Victorinoir* figures. Like the hard-boiled women in film noir, she is punished for her expression of desire by inflexible social conventions and the men around her, notably Mr. Tulkinghorne, Sir Leiscester Dedlock's solicitor, who personifies the callous and dehumanizing social institutions that characterize the modern world for Dickens.

In the novel, Dickens's language makes clear the threat of the lurking and hulking Mr. Tulkinghorn (with an "e" in the film), who is motivated by the desire to acquire power through the exploitation of other people's secrets. Tulkinghorn "wears his usual expressionless mask—if it be a mask—and carries family secrets in every limb of his body, and every crease of his dress" (151). Paralleling the perverse and corrupt male power brokers in film noir such as *Chinatown*'s Noah Cross and *Gilda*'s Ballen, Tulkinghorn is defined by his vampirish manipulation of the vulnerability of others. He lies in wait to impose threat and menace on those around him: "More impenetrable than ever, he sits, and drinks, and mellows as it were, in secrecy; pondering, at that twilight hour, on all the mysteries he knows" (284).

In Elvey's adaption, Tulkinghorne similarly exploits Lady Dedlock's secret—that she has had an affair with Captain Hawdon before she marries Sir Leicester, although she was told that the child of that romance, Esther Summerston, died in birth. While the film lacks Dickens's mythifying descriptions of Tulkinghorn, the solicitor in the film is similarly menacing in his devotion to rule and convention. For Tulkinghorne, "the honour of the Dedlocks is a religion," and thus he immediately grows suspicious of Lady Dedlock's dramatic reaction to the letter whose handwriting she recognizes as that of her (thought to be dead) lover from 18 years earlier, Captain Hawdon (now known as Nemo, "Nobody," "ragged, foul and filthy" [Elvey]).

The film shows Lady Dedlock to be victimized by Tulkinghorne's merciless devotion to "honour" at all costs, showing her role as "cold and haughty leader of society" to be the direct result of a brutal past. Although this is the extent of Elvey's reference to Lady Dedlock's coldness and mysteriousness (the rest of her story is cast very sympathetically in terms of Tulkinghorne's "hunting down" of her secret to expose her), Dickens outlines Lady Dedlock's anomie in more recognizably noir terms. She lives "in the desolation of Boredom and the clutch of Giant Despair" (143), and the contradiction of hopelessness, cynicism, and desire characterizes her affect, as it does most of film noir's leading characters. Her life is "detestable monotony" (13) and yet she carries some dark energy, becoming "restless, very restless" (202).

The novel also suggests a continuity among the interminable and arbitrary workings of Chancery, the ruthless victimization of the innocent (notably illustrated in the story of Jo), the foggy impenetrable and morally degenerated noir city, and the cruel fate of Lady Dedlock, whose experience, like that of the impotent Chancery, is of "a deadened world" (7):

> My Lady Dedlock's place has been extremely dreary. The weather, for many a day and night, has been so wet that the trees seem wet through . . . the vases on the stone terrace in the foreground catch the rain all day: and the heavy drops fall drip, drip, drip upon the broad flagged pavement, called, from old time, the Ghost's Walk, all night.
>
> (8)

Defined by the rainy noir setting that surrounds her, and haunted by the past, Dickens's hard-boiled Lady Dedlock "supposes herself to be an inscrutable Being, quite out of reach and ken of ordinary mortals" (11). Lady Dedlock's alienation is characterized by an affect symbiotically in keeping with her environment.

Elvey intermittently uses what we would now identify as strikingly noir visual terms in his adaptation, and the style highlights in particular the trauma of Lady Dedlock's *femme moderne*. Elvey's mise-en-scene is most striking in three noir sequences. The first serves as a refrain for the film. In a shot repeated three times, Elvey first marks Hawdon's death by framing the gated bars leading into the graveyard with an arch whose lamp hangs from its center. This lovely noir image, clearly derived directly from the drawings of Phiz, Dickens's illustrator, is invoked again when Lady Dedlock comes here with Jo; however, this time, Elvey then cuts to a shot of Lady Dedlock and Jo from the graveside, the characters seemingly now locked behind the bars they look through. The scene looks forward to the many shots in film noir of bars and gates symbolizing characters trapped and fated.[7] In Elvey's shot, there is no context or color, only darkness, outside the iris capturing the bars.

Elvey once more invokes the graveside shot at the end of the film, when Lady Dedlock falls at the steps of the arched gates, clinging to the bars. Elvey gives us first an establishing shot, then cuts in closer to Lady Dedlock holding on to the gate. The final shot of the film is here, with Lady Dedlock at the graveyard steps and Esther praying by her mother's side with bars behind her.

The graveyard scenes (Figures 4.2 and 4.3) prefigure a noir style while framing the story of a woman victimized by unbending gender and class laws, as does the murder scene, in which George goes to see Tulkinghorne at his flat to inquire about Hawdon. In this scene, George waits for Tulkinghorne to answer (he is not at home) and stands at the

Figure 4.2 "Consecrated Ground," *Bleak House* (1853), Phiz (Hablot K. Brown). (This image may be used without prior permission for any scholarly or educational purpose. Image scanned by George P. Landow; http://www.victorianweb. org/art/illustration/phiz/bleakhouse/11.html.)

right side of a shot of a stairwell framed by an arch. While George's shadow cuts diagonally across Tulkinghorne's door, a veiled woman in black sneaks up the stairs and hides in the shadows on the left across the hall from Tulkinghorne's door (we think the woman could be Lady Dedlock but learn later it is Hortense, the embittered French maid Lady Dedlock earlier fired for spying on her). After George leaves, the lawyer does return to his flat, and walks up the stairs, as the woman again slips into the shadows. Tulkinghorne enters his room, with the door behind him presumably still open, and the film cuts to an iris shot of a hand firing a gun into the lit room. We see Tulkinghorne drop, then the killer shuts the door and descends the chiaroscuro-lit stairwell. Elvey prefigures the noir style, using shadows and iconic emphases on

Figure 4.3   "The Morning," *Bleak House* (1853), Phiz (Hablot K. Brown). (This image may be used without prior permission for any scholarly or educational purpose. Image scanned by George P. Landow; http://www.victorianweb.org/art/illustration/phiz/bleakhouse/37.html.)

figures of murder and mystery ("the gun") to capture the desperation of individuals caught in the moral and social webs of modern existence.

The film highlights gender and class as the site of social misery, drawing out this *Victorinoir* aspect of Dickens's novel. That Lady Dedlock and Hortense share a possible role as murderer establishes a structural link between these women seemingly belied by their class differences and the hatred between them. However, both women are manipulated by Tulkinghorne and both feel trapped and are trying to better position themselves. Like Lady Dedlock, Hortense is treated with contempt by Mr. Tulkinghorne, who throws her a coin after she brings him the note hidden by Lady Dedlock about Jo's friendship with Nemo (Captain Hawdon). Later in the film, Detective Bucket discovers Jo and arranges a performance in Tulkinghorne's office to try to discover the truth about Lady Dedlock. Detective Bucket and Tulkinghorne dress Hortense up in Lady Dedlock's black clothes, the film again establishing a link between these two women marked—their reputations "blackened"—by their desires. Jo is asked to identify the woman in black, whom he escorted to Hawdon's gravesite. First he says that Hortense is that woman, but then he corrects himself. Jo has been educated by living on the city streets to notice visual details; here, he observes that Hortense doesn't wear the rings that Jo remembers "the veiled Lady in black" wearing ("she 'ad rings on wot sparkled"). As Jo makes his declaration, he is flanked by the representatives of the law and its enforcement—on the right, Detective Bucket, and on the left, a perversely jubilant Tulkinghorne shaking with glee, rubbing his hands together in an appetitive gesture of dominance, success, and knowledge. In the background stands Hortense, the black-dressed silent evidentiary pawn standing behind Jo. The mise-en-scene foreshadows Hortense's marginalization—although here she moves up to take Jo's place. Later in the film, when Hortense, "out of work and desperate, presses Mr. Tulkinghorne for more money," he ignores her. She says, "You use me as a tool! You fling me aside . . . ! I will be avenged!"

The film's emphasis on the story of these women brings into relief the *femme moderne*'s story, a *Victorinoir* dramatization, filtered from Dickens's as, once again, the most interesting ("For this picture," the titles begin, "we have chosen the most dramatic of all the tales embedded in the book—the story of the hunting down of Lady Dedlock, and the discovery of her secret"). Elvey's film highlights Lady Dedlock's noir story of failed female desire in the context of modernity's rigid social scripts. Further, if Dickens "dreamed" the cinema, as Grahame Smith argues in his book about Dickens's anticipation of film, the dreaming—as interested as it was in criminality, the labyrinthine dangers of the city, and the haunting psychosocial effects of class and gender—took a distinctly noir cast.

Hardy and *Victorinoir*

Thomas Hardy continues this Victorian dreaming of film noir's social conflicts and embattled gender identities. There is no better example of the tragic consequences for women and culture of rigid psychosocial gender expectations than is seen in Thomas Hardy's *Tess of the D'Urbervilles* (1891). The novel systematically posits and then criticizes the imagining of woman, alternately, as angel or "femme fatale." Hardy reveals Angel Clare's failure to see Tess beyond images; when he finds out that Tess has been raped and exploited by Alec D'Urberville, Angel remarks, "You were one woman and now you are another" (298). Tess internalizes this unmerciful reading of her self when she says, "She you love is not my real self but one in my image; the one I might have been" (281). Tess is caught and bound by those awful projections, as is Judy Barton in Hitchcock's noir film *Vertigo*. Judy is literally remade into the fictional Madeleine, first by Gavin Elster then by Scotty Ferguson. Although Scotty cruelly and absurdly repeats to Judy, "It can't matter to you," viewers maintain an identification with him because he is initially duped (though primarily by Elster and not the woman) and because he is played by James Stewart, whose star text promises virtue and middle-class morality. Despite Scotty's psychotic insistence on projecting an idea of woman onto Judy herself ("Couldn't you like me just the way I am?" Judy asks Scotty), the audience identifies with him. This identification signifies the perverse stubbornness of ideation about women and gender that appears *within* these texts, but that also extends to readers and viewers whose repetition of the controlling projection of the idea of the "femme" onto complex representations of female experience stymies their ability to read and interpret these texts well. The representation of women's stories and female autonomy is often submerged in discussions of the "femme fatale."

Hardy's interest in the gender problems resulting from the projection of narrow categories on offer is continued in *Jude the Obscure*, published four years after *Tess of the D'Urbervilles*. In this novel, Sue Bridehead's vexed psychological state and social condition are repeatedly made clear to Jude, but he insists that her behavior is not "natural." Just as Jeff Bailey refuses to acknowledge the real hard-boiled Kathy Moffett (in favor of a fantasy of her) in *Out of the Past*, Jude can't accept Sue's measured responses (Sue says, "I care for you as for anybody I ever met" [160]). Jude's difficulty accepting Sue's ambivalence recalls Pip's relation to Estella, the "femme fatale" figure in *Great Expectations*. Estella's schematic role in the novel as a projection of Pip's desires is conveyed in her warning to Pip that he is in love with an idea and not her self:

> "I have tried to warn you of this; now, have I not?"
> I said in a miserable manner, "Yes."
> "Yes. But you would not be warned, for you thought I did not mean it. Now, did you not think so?"
> "I thought and hoped you could not mean it. You, so young, untried, and beautiful, Estella! Surely it is not in Nature."
> "It is in *my* nature," she returned.
>
> (376)

Hardy's Jude Fawley shows similar blindness with regard to the woman he claims to love. That Sue rebels against female social roles Jude respects as an intellectual point, but when Sue refuses to be feminine and sexually available (such refusal coded in the novel as "capricious-ness" and "inconsistency," just as in film noir movies), Jude falls back on cultural stereotypes about deceitful and harmful woman:

> Or was Sue simply so perverse that she willfully gave herself and him pain for the odd and mournful luxury of practicing long-suffering in her own person, and of being touched with tender pity for him at having made him practice it? . . . Possibly she would go on inflicting such pains again and again, and grieving for the sufferer again and again, in all her colossal inconsistency.
>
> (189)

Although *Great Expectations* is clearly less interested in and enlight-ened about gender politics than are Hardy's novels, the logic of *Great Expectations* and *Jude the Obscure* makes available a feminist insight into the substitution of male fantasy for complex psychic and social female experience. This is why female characters in these novels seem to take the place of the free-floating desires of the male protagonists. Estella is an embodiment of Pip's illusory expectations, a surrogate representa-tion of money and class; Sue Bridehead is a surrogate for Christminster, the apogee of higher education to which Jude aspires. Jude, we are told, "[parts] his lips" as he addresses the Christminster wind: "'You,' he said, addressing the breeze caressingly, 'were in Christminster city between one and two hours ago, floating along the streets, pulling round the weather-cocks, touching Mr. Phillotson's face, being breathed by him; and now you are here breathed by me—you, the very same '" (19). One could argue that Sue is in fact an irrelevance, given the way the beginning of the passage posits the wind as a means of trafficking desire between the two male intellects—surely Sue's complex character interrupts and frustrates the flow of such desire. While Sue Bridehead becomes Jude's ostensible object of desire, Jude continues to express his erotic attachment to Christminster: "[Jude] was getting so romantically attached to Christminster that, like a young lover alluding to his mis-tress, he felt bashful at mentioning its name again" (20). Indeed, Jude's desires are cast in terms of his failure to measure up to other men, who have resources he lacks; Jude is "elbowed off the pavement by the mil-lionaires' sons" (161). A noir sentiment, both in its suggestion of com-petition among men and the idealist's turn to cynicism, the comment might well describe *Double Indemnity*'s Walter Neff. Like Jude, Walter Neff is seduced not just by a woman, Phyllis Dietrichson as the "femme fatale," but also by the homosocial fantasy that he can compete with Keyes ("I was trying to think with your brain, Keyes"; "It's something I had been thinking about for years").

James Naremore has explored the intriguing thesis that "the 'original' film noirs can be explained in terms of a tense, contradictory assimilation of high modernism into the American culture industry as a whole" (7). Modernist literature and film noir certainly share an interest in style (in Paul Schrader's words, "artistic solutions to sociological problems" [63]). They also both inherit some major Victorian conflicts about the representation of class and gender. As Philip Kemp has argued, class in noir is "no joke. It functions as an instrument of oppression, a cause of hatred and violence." Using *The Locket* as an example (another film, like the ones I discussed in Chapter 3, in which a woman's psychological illness represents social disorder), Kemp notes the way the *The Locket* "furnishes a mordant parable of the wealth-based class system, and the moral and psychological distortion inflicted on those who live in it" (82). In *Double Indemnity*, from Neff's point-of-view shot of a production-line office layout at the "Pacific All-Risk" company, to Neff's admission to Keyes that the murder/get-rich-quick scheme was something he'd been thinking about "for a long time," to the elevator operator's comment that he couldn't get insurance because of "something loose in the heart," the film repeatedly paints a portrait of modern life as a classist society that traps people in meaningless jobs so that their lives are drained of meaningful social interaction. It is notable that the "lovable" character in this film charms Wilder's audiences by showing what a slave to actuarial charts he is.

Walter Neff's homosocial desire, as is the case for Hardy's Jude, is activated by the awareness of an oppressive setting: for Jude, the limited possibilities on offer in rural Marygreen; for Neff, modern conformity, characterized by actuarial charts and cubicle office space. For both of these modern characters, idealism and desire frustrate them quite literally to death.

The vamp

In the years intervening between Victorian representations of "bad women" and film noir's "femmes fatales," silent film reconfigured the vampire as the cinema vamp, a shadow image of the *femme moderne* flapper figure. In the films of Theda Bara, for example, woman was presented as a sorceress who stole men's power to determine the fate of the self and community. As Janet Staiger has said about the representation of "bad women" in early American film, "[t]he vampire or spider image of sucking away the man's blood was a powerful metaphor for the threat she represented" (150).

As in the earlier literary medium and the later film noir explorations of gender distress in changing social periods, bad-women silent films such as *Traffic in Souls* (1913), *A Fool There Was* (1915), and *The Cheat* (1915), Staiger rightly says, "insist upon the value of a new independent, intelligent, and aggressive woman, even a *desiring* woman. Thus, the films are not simple instances of patriarchal repression of women" (xvi–xvii). Indeed these films present women cast as vampires and spiders subverting social norms and conventions designed to subdue and control them. In *A Fool There Was* (Frank Powell, 1915), we see a direct link between Victorian regulation of gender identities and Hollywood film, since the film was adapted from a play by Porter Emerson Browne inspired, first, by the Philip Burne-Jones painting "The Vampire," on view in 1897 (the year of Stoker's publication of *Dracula*) (Figure 4.4) and second, by the Rudyard Kipling poem "The Vampire" that was also inspired by the painting. Kipling's poem begins with the line Brown and later *A Fool There Was* used for their titles.

Figure 4.4   Philip Burne-Jones, "The Vampire" (1897).

Apart from an earlier film adaptation inspired by the painting and Kipling poem (Kalem's *The Vampire* [1913]), *A Fool There Was*, as James Card notes, was the most influential film to initiate an on-screen projection of the deadly seductress figure.

Like the sexualized Victorian literary heroines such as Lucy Westenra, Tess, and Estella, cast darkly to simplify gender politics, sexualized women in early film were similarly portrayed, in order to highlight the convention of Victorian female purity: "Early film," Card suggests, "inherited the heroines of the Victorian theatre. Their essential quality was purity. They were the noble women whom men were expected to place on pedestals and court only with poetry and romantic protestations of eternal devotion" (181). In contrast, in 1923, the fan magazine *Classic* called Bara the "red enemy of man . . . daughter of the new world . . . peasant . . . goddess . . . eternal woman" (Card, 189). Dawn Sova discusses how Theda Bara "slithered across pre-1920 screens in forty movies between 1916–1919 as 'The Vamp,' short for 'vampire'" (Sova, 21). And yet, as in Victorian literary representations of the "femme fatale" figure, the contexts of these representations often showed these characters to be feminist, or part of a feminist rebellion against conventional gender identities.

In *A Fool There Was*, the New Woman Elinor articulates a reasonable and sympathetic critique of the double standard that regulates gender roles: "You men shield each other's shameful sins. But were it a woman at fault, how quick you'd be to expose and condemn her." Elinor's feminist remark is paralleled in Geschwitz's defense of Lulu at the end of the court scene in *Pandora's Box* (1929), when Geschwitz attacks the smug prosecuting attorney: "Counselor, do you know what would have happened to your wife if, as a child, she'd had to spend her nights in cheap cafes?" While popular readings of Lulu cast her as a quintessential "femme fatale," the film shows the men to be the more dangerous source of violence. Schoen, with his menacing and intermittently shadowed gaze; the exploitative Marquis Casti-Piani; Roderigo; Lulu's "father" Schigolch; Alwa, the weak cohort; then, famously, Jack the Ripper—they are brutes, killers, exploiters, and fools, and Lulu, a *femme moderne* who really just wants to have fun, is trafficked among the men, until she's finally stabbed to death by Jack the Ripper. As Martin Esslin has said, "Lulu is a character of pristine *innocence*; it is society which is sick" (qtd. in Davidson, 47).

The packaging of these films about vamps prefigures the marketing of film noir "femmes fatales." Speaking of cultural representations of women in the Weimar period, Patrice Petro says that, "[t]o a certain extent, the representation of the modern woman was a projection of male anxieties and fears—anxieties and fears emanating from various phenomena of modernity that were recast and reconstructed in terms of an uncontrollable and destructive female sexuality" (34).

Sheri Chinen Biesen similarly catalogs the publicity advertisements that capitalized on the craving of American viewers for treacherous women. The publicity for *Murder My Sweet* (Edward Dmytryk, 1944) reads, "Don't fall for that feeling. . . . She kills like she kisses!" (Beisen, 115), and advertising for *The Postman Always Rings Twice* takes on the imagined perspective of a version of Garfield's character, overwhelmed by desire, announcing, "You must be a she-devil . . . you couldn't make me feel like this if you weren't" (Biesen, 122). Out-of-control men are repeatedly overshadowed by the demonized powerful and competent woman. Indeed, as Beisen notes in her discussion of *Gilda* (Charles Vidor, 1946), "[p]ublicity for *Gilda* reproaches strong, independent women as responsible for violent male behavior" (152). Petro's account of this phenomenon in the context of German culture suggests modernity, and particularly the modern city, figured as a seductive female: "this tendency to exaggerate in representing Berlin as a woman reveals less about women in Weimar than it does about a male desire that simultaneously elevates and represses woman as object of allure and as harbinger of danger" (43).

Jackie Stacey has written extensively about the complicated forms of identification produced between female spectators and Hollywood stars. Her book *Star Gazing: Hollywood Cinema and Female Spectatorship* devotes several chapters to analyzing the processes that governed female spectatorship in Britain during the 1940s and 1950s. In her discussion of the "reproduction of feminine identities in relation to cultural ideals" (227), Stacey points to the subversiveness inherent in female viewers' identification with on-screen actresses:

> The processes, and practices, which involve reproducing similarity seem to be those extra-cinematic identifications, which take place in the spectator's more familiar domestic context, where the star's identity is selectively reworked and incorporated into the spectator's new identity. Even in these cases, identification involves not simply the passive reproduction of existing femininities, but rather an active engagement and production of changing identities.
>
> (171)

Stacey's research and her extensive interviews with wartime and postwar female viewers reveal that these women experienced empowerment, as they saw dynamic versions of themselves on-screen. The processes of identification between female viewers and Hollywood stars can provide multiple and progressive opportunities for women to reimagine themselves:

> [T]he qualities of confidence and power are remembered as offering female spectators the pleasure of participation in qualities they themselves lacked and desired . . . . Hollywood stars can thus be seen as offering more than simple role models of sexual attractiveness (though clearly they offered this too!). However, they were also remembered as offering female spectators a source of fantasy of a more powerful and confident self.
>
> (158)

Stacey's analysis of the forging of "the spectator's new identity"—the prospect of "changing identities" during a time of gender instability and rapid social change—sheds light on the projection of fatality onto roles associated with female desire. If it is the case that, as Stacey says, "many forms of identification involve processes of transformation and production of new identities, combining the spectators' existing identity with her desired identity and her reading of the star's identity" (172), then surely it is in the perceived best interests of men and the status quo to control that reading. Projecting a categorical label such as the "femme fatale" onto female images of desire short-circuits the transformation Stacey implies is inherent in female spectators' relationship to these images.

Richard Dyer is also interested in spectator identification. In his fascinating discussion of the relationship between the spectator and the impact of star image on role and character, Dyer suggests the role of sympathy in contemporary viewer responses to Lana Turner, a point that complements my suggestion in Part I that Cora Smith is more of a subject in *The Postman Always Rings Twice* than critical and popular discussions of that film usually allow for: "the film is about Cora at least as much as it is about Frank" (Dyer, "Lana," 418). Dyer notes Cora Smith's impulsiveness, but also her entrapment and her ambition, complicating a simple view of Cora as the means of Frank's destruction:

> Thus if in terms of the relationship between the motivational and star image levels, Turner serves to mask the contradictions of the *femme fatale* type (a type, of course, that reflects the male construction—and fear of—the female), in terms of the relationship between the structural and star levels, Turner serves to open up the tension between what women are for men and what that means

for women as women. (I am not positing here any brilliance on Turner's part—though I would never wish to denigrate her performing abilities—or an untutored feminist sensibility on the part of the director, writer, or whoever; it is rather that in the relationship between her life/films and women audiences, a certain registering and defining of the female experience in this society was possible and that this happens in *Postman* simply because she is in it.)

(418)

Stacey's and Dyer's research and insights suggest a context for understanding the psychosocial associations that viewers draw between the Hollywood star and the desires of female viewers, which further helps to explain the tone of fascination and danger (as well as an intermittent cultural hysteria) that has circulated around cinematic images of strong women.

Louise Brooks's portrayal of Lulu fits squarely in the habitual pattern of projection and mystification, mythified as Brooks has been by critics. Adou Kyrou in *Amour-Erotisme et Cinema* wrote that "Louise is the perfect apparition, the dream woman without whom the cinema would be a poor thing. She is much more than a myth, she is a magical presence, a real phantom, the magnetism of the cinema" (qtd. in Card, 205). The mythifying of the female image carries with it the danger of objectifying powerful women as animalistically other, as in Sova's referencing of Theda Bara as having "slithered across pre-1920 screens." In the case of *Pandora's Box*, indeed, the predisposition has been to see the luminous portrayal of Lulu by Louise Brooks (Figure 4.5) and Pabst's claustrophobic yet radiant close-ups of Brooks as contributing to Lulu's narcissism and an unsettling and inexplicable seductiveness, her "cool, enigmatic charm" (Davidson, 33). However, *Pandora's Box* invites us *not* to share in the violent projection of lack and failure on the part of the men in the film onto Lulu but to criticize their failures and respond to Lulu's vivacity and beauty. Indeed, Patrice Petro provides a context for Lulu's vitality as a positive marker of female agency in popular German images of the modern woman: "when we turn to the magazines and films that made their appeal explicitly to women, it is indisputable that the representation of the modern woman did address women's experiences of modernity—their dissatisfactions with traditionally defined gender roles and their desire for a transformation of those roles" (36).

While Lulu isn't herself a feminist character, her story, in its disregard for the social script written by patriarchy and enforced by the men around her, is indeed feminist. Changing roles constantly, as Karin

Figure 4.5   Louise Brooks as Lulu in *Pandora's Box* (*Die Büchse der Pandora*) (1929), George Eastman House.

Littau suggests, Lulu is utterly transgressive. And because Lulu's agency is utterly untethered to social convention, it must, according to cultural norms, be destroyed diagetically and then extra-diagetically contained by means of bestial imagery, as is seen in Lotte Eisner's striking comments on Lulu:

> [Lulu's] face is so voluptuously animal that it seems almost deprived of individuality. In the scene with Jack the Ripper, this face, a smooth mirror-like disc slanting across the screen, is so shaded out and toned down that the camera seems to be looking down at some lunar landscape. (Is this still a human being—a woman—at all? Is it not rather the flower of some poisonous plant?)
>
> (qtd. in Doane, 1991, 153)

Somehow, placed in proximity to iconic serial killer Jack the Ripper, Lulu, for Eisner, is the "poisonous" one.

Louise Brooks herself rebelled against the control of her director Pabst (as she did against Hollywood, leaving films altogether in 1927). The oft-quoted chilling exchange between Brooks and Pabst toward the end of the filming of *Pandora's Box* is recorded and quoted in Brooks's autobiography and by Elsaesser: "'Your life is exactly like Lulu's,' [Pabst] said, 'and you will end the same way.' At that time, knowing so little of what he meant by 'Lulu,' I just sat sullenly glaring at him, trying not to listen. Fifteen years later, in Hollywood, with all his predictions closing in on me, I heard his words again—hissing back to me" (qtd. in Elsaesser, 34). Interestingly, the snake imagery here is appropriated by Brooks to signify the venomous treatment of her by Hollywood—a telling contrast to sexist fantasies about the vamp, a personified "slithering" Theda Bara, both Eve and the snake.

If there seems to Pabst and to others some cruel logic in spirited women being brutally killed, it shouldn't be a surprise that representations of women that subvert conventional authority structures elicit simplistic responses and labeling, such as branding them as "femmes fatales." In Hollywood, studio executives exploited publicity stunts to mythify Theda Bara, reportedly calling in phrenologists to confirm, "[n]ever in all my experience as a professional character reader have I gazed into a face portraying such wickedness and evil—such characteristics of the vampire and the sorceress" (Golden, 63). Such virulent responses surely justify the reading by actresses who have played "vamps" and "femmes fatales" of their roles as complex, psychological, and social—and, explicitly in the case of Theda Bara, as feminist. Said Bara in 1915, "The vampire that I play is the vengeance of my sex upon its exploiters. You see . . . I have the face of a vampire, perhaps, but the heart of a 'feministe'" (Figure 4.6) (qtd. in Staiger, 160).

Bara's comment reveals the politics of silent-cinema's vamp, who was, as Buszek argues, "symbolic of not just feminism's potential power to destroy the family and society, but also the ways in which it might positively introduce new ideas about both women's passion and men's frailty as gender roles fluctuated not independently, but in relation to one another" (161).

The culmination of the late-Victorian vampire, who became the vamp of silent cinema, is film noir's "femme fatale." Sheri Chinen Beisen alludes to a Press book publicity image of *The Postman Always Rings Twice*, part of whose tagline I quoted early in this chapter. Here it is in its entirety: "A caricature of a huge hand cleaves a butcher knife above the tagline: 'Her name is Cora . . . . *She Gets Into Men's Blood . . . And Stays There! His name is Frank . . . His Savage Boldness Will Thrill the Women!'*" (123). Parasitic images of excess, blood-sucking, and contamination are apt vehicles for expressing contemporary anxieties about female power and transgression, resurfacing metaphors, as we have seen, that derive from Victorian vampire narrative. As women gain validation as part of the working population and the sexuality of women is expressed outside the strictly circumscribed spheres of prostitution

Figure 4.6   Vamp Theda Bara, BFI.

and domesticity, fiction and film work to articulate, grapple with, and in some cases contain female power and independence. As Biesen says, "The representation of independent, transgressive "femme fatales" and complex career women coincided with a wartime female labor force, nationally and inside the film industry" (125).

By offering strong and vital modern women, familiarly called "femmes fatales," who often gain our sympathy through their struggle to assume independence, film noir destabilizes gender categories, as did silent cinema's vamp, and allows us to see more clearly the reception of Victorian conceptions of class and gender in present-day popular culture and academic discourse, as well as the ongoing force of binary oppositions in the presentation and understanding of gender in contemporary culture. Such analysis exposes the extent to which we may be repressing film noir's past and helps us to come to a greater understanding of how cultural ideation about women informs our reading of, as well as writing about and filming, their experience, then and now.

Her authentic experience trumped by gender myths, Rita Hayworth once famously claimed that "[e]very man I knew went to bed with Gilda . . . and woke up with me." In her discussion of "Shakespeare's Sister" in *A Room of One's Own* (1929), Virginia Woolf gave voice to the phantom women elided by biased social conventions. Woolf wished to adumbrate, give outline to, the talented women who had not been acknowledged in canonical narratives. Analysis of misreadings of women in noir and a fuller understanding of the historical backdrops that inform our reception of them helps us similarly to outline the missing sisters of Gilda.

5
Looking Forward: Deconstructing The "Femme Fatale"

In this chapter, I'll be talking principally about David Lynch's *Mulholland Drive* (2001), although I include a fairly extensive study of Billy Wilder's *Sunset Boulevard* (1950), an original-cycle film noir text that certainly influenced Lynch's film significantly. I want to end with a discussion of *Mulholland Drive* because I believe it points toward unraveling some of the problems with representations of female agency I've addressed throughout this study. *Mulholland Drive* takes on the project of deconstructing the "femme fatale" figure and provides a filmic instance of what I think needs to be done in reimagining the relationship between feminist representation and female agency, as well as a cultural discourse suspicious of and resistant to both kinds of expression.

Just after Betty Elms's brilliant audition in *Mulholland Drive* (2001), casting agent Linney James (Rita Taggert) ushers Betty (Naomi Watts) to the sound stage where Adam Kesher (Justin Theroux) is casting for his new film, a part Linney tells Betty she "would kill—." The scene occurs as part of Diane Selwyn's dream of an alternate life for herself, as the sunny aspiring actress Betty Elms, and the brilliant Freudian truncation, lopping off the preposition "for" at the end of the sentence, serves to evoke the double reality of Diane's desire and ambition on the one hand and her rage at Adam for "stealing" her lover Camilla on the other. David Lynch captures in this moment not only the insufficiency of conventional "waking" syntax to attend to reality—an endorsement of different kinds of knowing, addressed, as I argued in Chapter 3, by such earlier film noir movies as *Whirlpool*—but also the propensity for the mind to fill experience in with language and images that meet needs— here, Diane's desperate and angry feelings of loss about her career and her lover. The moment seems to me emblematic of the clever, the imaginative, and the dangerous possibilities embedded not only in individual psychological projections but also in psychosocial projections that have real effects. As I've been arguing throughout, viewers and critics employ the "femme fatale" figure as a way of thinking about female agency that fills a social psychological need to contain female energy and sustain the status quo with regard to gender roles.

Mulholland Drive has evoked narrow responses in terms of its representation of women, with viewer reactions limited by our habit of processing Hollywood conventions without attending to the film's treatment of them. Here, I believe, Lynch employs the roles that women generally portray in film, playing them first for humor, but then revealing the tragic humanity of lives molded and finally destroyed by those roles constructed and consumed by a culture obsessed with celebrity. *Mulholland Drive* is a story about a depressed, jealous, failing actress called Diane Selwyn (Naomi Watts). When Diane's lover, Camilla Rhodes (Laura Harring), jilts her and taunts her by encouraging Diane to watch her with her new lover, a young self-important director named Adam Kesher, Diane contracts for her to be murdered. Presumably, Diane is so tormented by guilt after she has had Camilla killed that she shoots herself, the image that ends the movie but that begins a final moment of fantasy of Diane's that recasts her experience in LA and her affair with Camilla in utterly transformed ways. This dream story begins the film, and so we don't know until the end of the film why the film begins the way it does.

In following a tradition of films that question the medium and the Hollywood dream factory, *Mulholland Drive* provides a searing and effective critique of the failures of the dream factory to sustain the people seduced by it—and further suggests that these failures extend to a cruel indifference to female desire. I believe that *Mulholland Drive* levels its attack by way of the figure of the "femme fatale" and the conventions of representing women in film noir. Lynch takes the figure of the "femme fatale" and shows how the propagation of images of women and images of female desire, like the propagation of images of LA as a city of dreams, has a kind of currency in the culture that eviscerates the people seduced by that power.

Many have focused on *Mulholland Drive*'s allusion to the good girl/bad girl motifs familiar to film viewers: referring to the women in the film, Ruby Rich calls it "as she sees it," identifying "[o]ne, blond, one brunette, one innocent, one not" [45]). In contrast, I think that David Lynch's visceral brain-teasing film is a deeply feminist reworking of gender typography in order to endorse an imaginative openness with regard to experience. Analysis of the film has argued for the "various logics," in David Andrews's terms, of the film's narrative, as well as for and against reading the film as coherent and teleological. I believe, in line with Andrews's reading, that the film has *both* a narrative coherence and an openendedness, but I want to go beyond that too to suggest an understanding of such openendedness as thematic and as deeply humanist, rather than just aesthetic.

Invoking Rita's "tabula rasa" presence in the film, Jennifer Hudson articulates *Mulholland Drive*'s prioritizing of emotional intuitive knowledge and "the fluidity and promise that comes from not having a fixed self," values that are traditionally feminist, in the terms that I was discussing in relation to *Whirlpool* in Chapter 3. Hudson rightly says that Lynch "takes his mistrust of intellectual discourse, defers it by showing its illusiveness, and then uses emotional responses as a fluid and sexual language that expresses what words cannot" (23). However, Hudson sees Lynch's appreciation of the affective order as an aesthetic investment, while I want to suggest that this "new mode of making sense" (Hudson, 23) constitutes a powerful argument for imaginative flexibility in engaging the world, a relinquishing of the judgment that attends to labeling and categorization. Thus as in Ann's intuitive resistance to Korvo in *Whirlpool*, her mind and body's unconscious rebellion against the oppressive gender roles on offer in the "torture chamber called Mrs. William Sutton," *Mulholland Drive*, more pointedly than the earlier film, presents the affective unconscious mode as a more reliable means of understanding. For Lynch, affect and receptivity are valued as a means of making human connection; moments of empathy and heightened consciousness hold in abeyance the alienation brought about by social institutions inattentive to the bad gender ideology they perpetuate. Lynch is interested in showing the extent to which cultural establishments are at odds with creativity, awareness, and human compassion, and one of the central ways he explores this disjunction is by invoking the figure of the "femme fatale" in order to deconstruct it.

While the film may seem to titillate as a result of its reliance on the noir icon of the fatal woman, in fact *Mulholland Drive* gains its power from its deconstruction of the idea of the "femme fatale" in favor of empathy and an affective orientation to trauma. The trauma here is linked to the brutality of the American dream machine as it is expressed in cultural obsessions with celebrity. The film lures us into the fantasy of the American dream, then rips apart the illusion, leaving us with a tragic story about disappointment, disillusionment, desperation, and suicide.

Although *Mulholland Drive* is an unameliorative film about failed desire, one of the strange fascinations of the film, as is the case in all of David Lynch's work, is its insistence on the value of moments of heightened perception. Lynch inherits a deeply modernist view of experience and art. He finds meaning in discrete acts of the imagination, moments of consciousness and the specific operations of the unconscious. In the context of making films and of watching them, Lynch's attitude is indeed that of literary modernism, a commitment to representing within his films the relationship between art and images, intractable realities, and the moments of perception and human connection that stave off the general violence of experience.

Such belief in the power of the mind to produce and receive meaningful stimuli registers human potential for Lynch that works against the film's cynicism. As Martha Nochimson suggests in her emphasis on Lynch's hopefulness, "an optimism that most critics overlook" (*Film Quarterly*, 39), *Mulholland Drive* responds to the brutal exploitation it explores: first, in the soothing dream logic of the Betty story, whose psychological "sense" fulfills our desire to impose narrative patterns on the images we see; second, in the film's modeling of the flexibility of identity, mainly demonstrated in the uncanny performance of Naomi Watts as Betty/Diane. Watts's assuming of identities, in her acting the parts of Betty and Diane, as well as the erotic role she plays in Betty's "audition," suggests an openness to experience that belies the rigidity and authority that characterize Hollywood's power structure and the patriarchal projection of labels onto *femmes modernes* struggling to be active in the social world.

Mulholland Drive models a way of using the "femme fatale" figure as a critical tool, as a means of understanding the vexed relationship between vital female agency and the limits placed on female desire and ambition by the patriarchal ideology that inhabits social institutions. The film actively deconstructs the "femme fatale" image by dissecting it as one of a number of projections of desire that results in the victimization of women. The movie doesn't posit a good girl/bad girl opposition, as some critics have stated; rather, the film, like many film noir movies before it, reveals the artificiality of such images of women and their destructiveness to individuals.

Echoing *Sunset Boulevard*'s scathing critique of Hollywood opportunism and the destruction of innocence, *Mulholland Drive* offers trenchant commentary on the extent to which Hollywood churns women up and punctures their dreams and their compassion. Critics have noted the similarities between *Mulholland Drive* and *Sunset Boulevard*: the exposure of vulgar opportunism, the physical evocation of Billy Wilder's 1950 film in *Mulholland Drive*'s street signs, courtyards, and the iconic entrance to

Paramount Studios; the "conflation of death and life" (Nochimson, *Film Quarterly*, 40); and the well-documented affection Lynch has expressed for the earlier film. Certainly the two films are points on a continuum of some of the best American films made about the American dream, Los Angeles, and Hollywood, including Robert Altman's 1992 film *The Player* and Curtis Hanson's *LA Confidential* (1997). The latter, an expose of the dark underbelly of the American Dream, begins with Detective Budd White's observation of domestic violence. Both Budd's rage and the violence he witnesses raise the specter of suppressed anger, violence sublimated into a sanitized set of images (alluded to ironically in Budd's surname) about opportunity and success: the Hollywood dream masking the American nightmare.

While such films share a virulent critique of the idea of the American Dream as it is instantiated by Hollywood, *Sunset Boulevard* and *Mulholland Drive* are particularly interested in the plight of women, as they reflect the cultural demand for, restrictions on, and destructive manipulation of the female image. *LA Confidential* addresses the idea in Lynn Bracken's having been remodeled into Veronica Lake and Susan Lefferts into Rita Hayworth; the women in the film are killed or exploited by corrupt men who employ images of women interchangeably with individual women themselves. In this way, the film considers the connection between the "dream" city of LA and illusory projections onto woman. Both LA and Woman are figured as cultural spaces filled by destructive collective fantasies and projections of desire that sustain male power, parodied in *LA Confidential* in Officer Jack Vincenne's popular status as "Celebrity Crime-Stopper." In this regard, it is interesting that Michael Chion refers to the abstracted power-broker Mr. Roque in *Mulholland Drive* as "a Doctor Mabuse hiding in his lair" (215), since Fritz Lang's "master criminal" is another noir expression of the perverse forms absolute control can take, and both Lang and Lynch are deeply interested in the consequences of masculine power for women.[1]

In *Mulholland Drive*, we see the idea of Los Angeles linked specifically with a fantasy about ambition and the Hollywood dream. As Vernon Shetley has said, we share with Diane the position "of being an outsider, observing and fantasizing about the glamorous star beyond our reach" (121). Such ideation about the Hollywood dream is beautifully rendered in the opening sequence of *Mulholland Drive*. The film begins with Diane's dream alter ego, Betty Elms, jitterbugging her way to win a contest that allows her to come to Hollywood to realize her aspiration to be an actress: as Betty later says to Rita (Diane's dream version of Camilla), "I just came here from Deep River, Ontario, and now I'm in this dream place." The film establishes a continuity between Diane's fantasy version of herself, Betty, who comes out of the "deep river" of Diane's unconscious, and the cultural myth of Hollywood as a dream place where "stars are ageless," as Norma says in *Sunset Boulevard.* Indeed, just as Norma is described by Cecil B. DeMille to have been a sweet young thing when she gained her fame in silent movies, Betty is portrayed as optimistic, bright, and utterly untouched by cynicism.

Betty's hopefulness and excitement about the opportunity of becoming a star are captured in the resonant mise-en-scene when she arrives at Paramount for her audition. The entrance is iconic, thanks to Norma Desmond's reception at the gates by Jonesy the security guard (who, dazed by Norma's "return," repeats, "Why it's Miss Desmond!"). The high-angle shot of Betty's arrival in the 2001 film enhances the tone of innocent aspiration, and Betty's buoyancy is further emphasized in Naomi Watts's affect, a go-get-em attitude that summons up the successful and beautiful women of 1970s Charlie perfume commercials, as well as Mary Tyler Moore's girl "Who can take the world on with her smile" from the same era. At the same time, I think some critics overstate Lynch's invocation of Hollywood clichés in the character of Betty Elms. George Toles, for example, says that "'Betty' is a character so entrenched in naivete and the hokey paraphernalia of small-townness that her whole confected being is a hymn to unreality" (3).

While Toles is certainly right that "Betty" calls to mind an assortment of well-rehearsed popular images (many citing Nancy Drew as a touchstone), I think the film is more interested in Betty than such a comment suggests.[2] For Betty is played with such engagement and openness by Naomi Watts that the performance seems to transcend the simple categories we want to impose on Betty.

Later in the film, as Betty and Rita nestle into bed together, Betty says, with disarming directness, "I'm in love with you." Betty's innocence and simplicity serve two functions in the film: first, Betty's incorruptibility contrasts with the manipulative workings of everyone in the Diane portion of the film, sharply revealing the brutality of the latter; second, Betty's artlessness sets up the film's exploration of performance (Watts's here, then later in the role of Diane, as well as Betty's spectacular audition performance) as an antidote to the poisons of contemporary Hollywood, female vitality exceeding the terrible limits of real experience and the formulaic conventions that dominate behavior and the professional workings of Hollywood. Female energy thus takes the place in this film of any specific role—"femme fatale" or "good girl"—invoked by the performances. While the film is replete with references to iconic women in Hollywood and Hollywood films (Lee Grant and Ann Miller, of course, as well as the evocation in Betty and Rita's lovemaking scene of Alma and Elizabeth in Bergman's *Persona* [1966]; Scotty's refashioning of Judy into Madeleine in *Vertigo*, as Rita is "remade" into a blonde), these gestures undermine rather than complete rigid identification with any one female role or type.

Mulholland Drive continually shifts its frame of reference, valuing an appreciation for evocation and flexibility in ascribing meaning to the images in the film. Rita is transformed, as is Judy Barton in Hitchcock's *Vertigo* (notably, Betty, the fantasy woman of Diane's dreams, wears a gray suit that calls to mind Madeleine's gray suit in *Vertigo*, Madeleine the fantasy woman of Scotty Ferguson's dreams), but the context differs. Unlike Scotty Ferguson, Betty protects and cares for Rita, which makes the disappearance of Betty and Rita and their supportive and nonironic bond register as a profound loss not just to us viewers, but also, obviously, to Diane Selwyn, whose experience of the loss finally culminates in her suicide.

Thus *Mulholland Drive* invokes the "femme fatale," the dangerous seductive woman, but not as an end in itself. The film's treatment of women belies Rich's schematic rendering of the "one innocent and one not" model quoted earlier, which works neither on the level of the dream nor the real, since the grounds for labeling the female characters in such a way keep shifting. Rita becomes a blonde. Diane repeats Camilla's call to her assassins on the widening road that traverses the Hollywood Hills, "We don't stop here." The blonde waitress in Winky's diner is called Diane, triggering associations for Rita that she is connected to or may herself be someone called Diane Selwyn. The film's language and images echo other moments within the film, but also a frame of reference outside the film having to do with victimized women, actresses in particular, with whose "power and insignificance," as Nochimson describes Lynch's women, viewers are familiar (Sheen and Davison, 166).

This film's diagetic and extradiagetic echoes thus create an alternate realm of language, images, and an imaginative rendering of connectedness, achieved through association and allusion. Such allusion achieves a richness of affect, since meaning accrues in an inchoate modernist way, evoking, as Conrad explains in *Heart of Darkness*:

> the meaning of an episode[,] not inside like a kernel but outside, enveloping the tale which brought it out only as a glow brings out a haze, in the likeness of one of these misty halos that sometimes are made visible by the spectral illumination of moonshine.
>
> (68)

Conrad's sense of meaning as adumbration captures Lynch's achieve-ment of an aesthetic and emotional resonance and richness of affect; however, as I suggested above, these moments in the film echo and refer back to a cultural pattern of the victimization of women. The invocation of the "femme fatale," in the context of a film that offers an alternative way of thinking about gender and sex roles as unfixed, becomes a tool for understanding the brutality of the cultural traps set for women who are caught up in the extreme categorization that reifies their experience.

It should be seen as no coincidence that in *Sunset Boulevard*, Norma Desmond seeks to resurrect Salome, the biblical young woman who is said in the New Testament to have caused the death of John the Baptist. The Salome echoed in the film is Oscar Wilde's 1896 *Victorinoir* Salome, who, desiring John the Baptist, had his head severed for spurning her. Salome figures as a compelling link between the late-Victorian *femme moderne* and film noir's women. Showalter quotes Carol Schorske's labe-ling of Salome as "the *fin de siecle*'s favorite phallic woman" (149), and Jane Marcus links Wilde's Salome with the New Woman (specifically Ibsen's Nora in *A Doll's House*), highlighting their resistance to male ritual and dominance in the form of a creative act, dance (105). For Marcus, the play is "a parable of the woman artist's struggle to break free of being the stereotype of sex object" (qtd. in Showalter, 156).

Similarly, John Paul Riquelme persuasively argues that Wilde's Salome breaks down the objectifying masculine gaze. She appropriates male power (in her rhetoric and in her control of the gaze) and serves to destabilize gender categories. Riquelme's interest in Sarah Bernhardt's role in bringing Salome to the stage is especially interesting, in relation to Norma Desmond's rewriting of Salome's story:

> As a young character realized by an actress who is no longer young, as a female character portrayed by a woman known for her male roles, and as a female character who mimics the language used by a man toward a woman, Salome does not exhibit herself to invite an exploitative gaze. Instead, by reversing our expectations, Salome looks back at us and makes possible a reevaluation of those expectations.
>
> (586)

Riquelme's understanding of Wilde's play illuminates in Salome a *Victorinoir* figure (in addition to *Great Expectation*'s Miss Havisham) standing behind Norma Desmond. Further, Salome herself is inflected by the dramatic flourishes of another performer: Bernhardt, a *femme moderne* who achieved a "studied and astonishingly successful manipulation of society's expectations" (Riquelme, 588). Bernhardt was unconventional and clever, a feminist icon for her contemporaries who were enthralled and, in some cases, disturbed by her possession of the roles she played:

> This clear construction of the characters bent to the will of the actress that conjured them—rather than vice versa—was threatening to many in this period of theater history, who preferred their dramatic actress's complete submission to not only the character she played, but also by extension the (overwhelmingly male) playwrights from which they originated.
>
> (Buszek, 122)

Bernhardt was 50 when she played Salome on stage, just as Norma is 50 when she seeks to resurrect Salome, both actresses seeking to "challenge and change," in Riquelme's words, the beleaguered status of female artists and actresses. Salome via Bernhardt shares, for Riquelme, Wilde's subversive view of gendered role-playing. For Norma Desmond's character, Salome may also be imagined through the lens of two *femme moderne* silent-film renderings: Theda Bara's "vamp" performance of Salome in the 1918 film of the same name and Russian actress Alla Nazimova's performance of the role in 1922. According to Showalter, "Although she was forty-four years old, [Nazimova] starred as a Salome who was very much an It Girl of the 1920s" (163), translating Salome's subversive female energy into the popular image of a Hollywood glamour girl. The references bespeak Salome's cultural function as a touchstone for gender flexibility, female creativity and subversiveness, and transvestitism. In one instantiation of the Salome story, *Sunset Boulevard* was reimagined and restaged in Greenwich Village in 1994 by the Mesopotamian Opera Company as *Sunset Salome*, a transvestite opera told from the point of view of Norma in the asylum, the vital woman struggling to manipulate or transform the grounds of her trapped existence.

Unlike Diane Selwyn, the *femme moderne* who dreams an escape from her miserable experience in Hollywood, Norma Desmond lives into middle age, but instead of dying tragically, she descends into madness, the film suggests, because she has been, like Dickens's Miss Havisham, "given the go by"—in this case by the Hollywood dream factory uninterested in aging women. Cecil B. DeMille, famous director of Biblical epics like *The Ten Commandments* and *Samson and Delilah* (and a filmmaker who, unlike Gloria Swanson and Erich Von Stroheim, made a successful transition from silent to sound movies), makes the point as he plays himself in the film. Norma mistakes DeMille's interest in her antique car for an interest in directing Norma in her comeback—or "return," as she puts it. (In response to "comeback," she says, "I hate that word! It's return!") When his assistant on the movie set asks, do you want me to "give [Norma] the brush," De Mille says, "Thirty million fans have given her the brush. Isn't that enough?" Norma's position in the film is keyed not so much to her role as a fatal woman but to the perverse and compelling excessive gestures that characterize her, certainly a more energetic response to victimization and a desperate sense of loss than any simple labeling of "femme fatale" evokes. As Nochimson says of the women in David Lynch's film, "[t]his electrifying female has crucial implications for the survival of the creative moment, a theme of abiding importance to Lynch" (Sheen and Davison, 165). Nochimson's account of Lynch's female characters applies equally to the excessive and vibrant Norma Desmond.

That *Mulholland Drive* wants to imagine strategies for women struggling to survive and succeed in Los Angeles can be seen in the Hollywood Hills setting's evocation of the story of Peg Entwistle, the "ghost" of Hollywoodland, as she was known in 1932, when actress Entwistle, depressed about her prospects for making it in the film industry, climbed the giant "H" and threw herself off the 50-foot "Hollywood" sign. Chased by the same demons that would later beset Norma Desmond and Diane Selwyn, Peg Entwistle had no resources other than the illusory dreams of success that fuel the star system. That Diane's story is to be seen in the context of a legacy of women ill-treated by Hollywood is suggested by Jay Lentzner and Donald Ross when they point out that Diane's surname alludes to Samuel Goldwyn and the Selwyn brothers, patriarchs who built the Hollywood empire. It is also worth noting that *Mulholland Drive* is dedicated to Jennifer Syme, an actress best known for being Keanu Reeves's long-term girlfriend but who was Lynch's assistant and appeared in Lynch's *Lost Highway*; she died in a car accident at the age of 28.

Given these resonances, it should be no surprise that David Lynch considered making a film about Marilyn Monroe. Lynch was drawn, here again, to "the idea of this woman in trouble," but, he continues, "I didn't know if I liked it being a real story" (Rodley, 268). Lynch prefers evocation and resonance, modes of representation I am saying serve aesthetic ends but also a feminist critique. Lynch is drawn to Monroe, as he is to Norma Desmond and Diane Selwyn, because he is interested in women's psychological responses to serving the Hollywood dream machine. "Consider," says Nochimson,

> the hordes of very young women who come and go as flavor of the month, objects of desire on whom hundreds of inconsequential, money-making films depend, and we must acknowledge how much hinges on the exploitation of this disposable figure whose energy briefly attracts and enchants.
>
> (Sheen and Davison, 166)

Chris Rodley, the editor of *Lynch on Lynch*, comments on the effects of such exploitation on actresses in connection with Marilyn Monroe's borderline personality. Monroe was "emotionally unstable, excessively impulsive and dependent on constant external approval" (269). While such a description fits in with Linehan's theory of validation in female borderline personalities, as discussed in Chapter 3, I think that Lynch is also aware of the cultural use to which Marilyn Monroe was put. As the actress herself said very eloquently, "I was always bumping into people's unconscious" (qtd. in MacCannell, 126). Hollywood in many ways epitomizes the "invalidating environment" to which Marsha Linehan attributes borderline personality disorder in women. Because Hollywood is, as Chris Rodley notes, "a place where everyone dreams of being someone—or something—else," the danger of losing the self in violent ways to "invalidating" forces (well exemplified in the evil corporate figures and thugs that people the setting in *Mulholland Drive*) is pervasive. Linehan's portrait illuminates the trauma and ultimate suicide of Diane, chased by little monsters generated by her superego:

> [T]he borderline individual adopts the emotionally invalidating attitude herself, often in an extreme manner, oversimplifying the ease of achieving behavioral goals and emotional goals. The inevitable failure associated with such excessive aspirations is met with shame, extreme self-criticism, and self-punishment, including suicidal behavior. The person deserves to be the way she is. The suffering she has endured is justified because she is so bad.
>
> (Linehan, 74)

Further, Lynch's disavowal of the borders between consciousness and the unconscious prompts an examination of cultural projections onto women and the dire consequences of having too smug a conviction about what we know and can control. In this light, Nochimson's description of the characters played by Laura Harring is intriguing. Rita is revealed to be "Hollywood's deadly, powerful, but utterly insignificant exploited girl: lethal, but always a pawn" (Sheen and Davison, 173). That the film blurs the boundaries among these women suggests the importance of this insight, one that questions our unexamined assumptions about who's in control, about our "use" of female images such as the "femme fatale."

Summoning up the tone of *Sunset Boulevard* in its mocking treatment of the conditions of possibility for women in Hollywood, *Mulholland Drive* extends tremendous sympathy to its heroines while sending up its own frame of reference. Both films pay tribute to and satirize the large-gestured flourishes of Hollywood celebrity. In *Sunset Boulevard*, for example, "We didn't need dialogue," Norma intones about the silent-movie era:

> We had faces. They opened their mouths and what came out: words, words, words. Well, you've made a rope out of words and strangled this business!

In the same exchange, when Joe says to Norma, "You used to be big," she replies, "I am big; it's the pictures that got small"—a veiled reference, as Robert Stam points out, to the growing popularity of television. Such melodramatic figuration, culminating in Norma's desperate call to Joe not to leave her—"Don't hate me! Don't stand there hating me"—posits Norma as a generic ghost, a silent-movie star in love with a guy from another kind of movie, noir protagonist Joe Gilles. When Joe looks at the inscription on the lighter Norma has given him, "Mad about the boy," the cruel humor of the clash of melodrama and noir is made clear, the unironized sentiment further parodied in Joe's and Betty Schaefer's mocking goodbye at Artie's New Year's party: "You'll be waiting for me?" "With a wildly beating heart." "Life can be beautiful."

Just as Norma's large gestures and utter lack of irony can't find purchase in Joe's fatalistic and opportunistic noir world (the clash evident in Figure 5.1), Betty Elms is similarly out of touch with the world that characterizes the Real in Lynch's film: male thugs, corporate exploiters, Hollywood egomaniacs, sycophants, and hack writers and directors working on clichéd biopic projects like "The Sylvia North Story," the real backdrops for Betty's dream naivete and optimism. Our sympathy for Diane, says Vernon Shetley, "offers a critique of Hollywood, its fierce and yet debilitating obsession with masculinity" (123).

Deflating Betty's and mad Norma's claims that the "stars are ageless," aging stars haunt *Mulholland Drive*, in the appearance of Robert Forster,

Figure 5.1 Melodrama meets film noir in *Sunset Boulevard* (1950) © Paramount Pictures. All rights reserved. Courtesy of Paramount Pictures. BFI.

Lee Grant, and Ann Miller, all traces of Hollywood past. Chad Everett, the dream-y Joe Gannon from *Medical Center*, becomes "Woody" Katz, the ageing roué Betty auditions with. Like Buster Keaton, Anna Nilson, and HB Warner in Norma's bridge game, Woody is one of the "wax works," his smarmy affect and over-tanned skin highlighting the effect. Coco's surname evokes the noir setting Lynch is fascinated by: "Ms. Lenoix—it is Mrs. Lenoix, is it?" Betty asks. Coco's response, "in all my living glory, baby," further evokes a cliché of Hollywood's golden big-screen fantasies, as the film plays with the idea of projected collective fantasies and individual trauma, the latter nicely evoked in Gene (Billy Ray Cyrus) the Pool Guy's appeal to Adam when the latter finds him in bed with his wife: "Just forget you ever saw it. It's better that way."

Our awareness of the various roles these characters and actors play in the film, like the mind-bending appearances of Gloria Swanson, Erich Von Stroheim, Cecil B. DeMille, and Hedda Hopper in *Sunset Boulevard*, is a response to *Mulholland Drive*'s preoccupation with absence and presence, the power of performance to summon up unlikely apparitions, and the value of being able to hold competing "realities" in our minds simultaneously, the "logics," as Andrews says, "which require viewers to hold multiple understanding in suspense." The film's undoing of the idea of fixed identities, fixed character roles, is, indeed, most pointedly seen, not just in Rita's status as "tabula rasa," but more richly in Betty's audition scene referenced above, which features a tour-de-force performance by Naomi Watts.[3] Watts transforms herself from ingénue to sultry seductress, underscoring not only, as Shetley notes, "the vividness of Diane's imagination," but also the artificiality and constructedness of female roles, the female image. In this scene, not only is Betty seducing Woody; Lynch seduces us to see beneath the innocent "Betty" to rehearse our familiar cultural response to Watts as a dangerous sexpot, as a "femme fatale." And yet, Watts "accomplishes the impossible"; as Todd McGowan says of Betty's audition performance:

> She is innocent yet sexual; she is naïve yet aware of how the world works; she is hopeful yet not easily duped. In short, Betty occupies subject positions that are contradictory and mutually exclusive.
>
> (77)

McGowan sees this flexibility as only possible because Betty is Diane's fantasy version of herself. The dream of woman—as sex kitten, as good-girl Betty (a reference to nice-girl Betty Schaefer in *Sunset Boulevard*?) is on offer to be analyzed, understood as a performance that could have variegated meanings, depending on the context.

Nochimson suggests something cathartic and wonderful about Betty's performance, a creative act that seems transcendent:

> Her reading creates something—a dangerously erotic mood—out of absolutely nothing. The lines Betty is given are utterly clichéd, the directions she receives from the director are meaningless, and her scene partner is made up of equal parts of snake oil and suntan. Her triumphant seizure of victory from the jaws of inanity is a distillation of the lowest form of the "magic" of mass-market movies, a chemistry that appears out of the blue without either warning or significance.
>
> (*Film Quarterly*, 41)

The seizure of victory is analogous to Norma's Chaplin impersonation, an unlikely register of Norma's ingenuity and talent that Joe Gilles is too cynical to register as anything other than a bafflement.

Elizabeth Cowie's analysis of the multiple roles available to women as film spectators, like Jackie Stacey's focus on the transformative quality of spectator identification, illuminates *Mulholland Drive*'s emphasis on the variegated possibilities on offer in the representation of women in film. Watts's portrayal of Betty employs such radically different tools from those used in her portrayal of Diane that the women seem physically distinct. As if to appropriate, then literalize, the classic hard-boiled detective cynicism we viewers recognize as the affect of a disappointed idealist, Watts gives us both turns and links bitter disillusionment with the optimism it presumably began as.

Norma Desmond and Betty are both out of time, ghosts of a more generous and receptive reality that we see through the glass darkly in the wonderment that surrounds the layers of performances by all of the actresses portrayed by and portraying Betty, Diane, Norma, Naomi, and Gloria. Norma is trapped in a fantasy of her earlier celluloid self (the young vibrant girl Cecil B. DeMille tells his assistant about at Paramount). The allusion to Norma's past resonates with our knowledge of Gloria Swanson's past: at the peak of her success, Swanson was enormously popular and extremely powerful. According to Buszek, Swanson not only gained fame playing women who "enjoyed freedoms and a lifestyle far beyond the reach of the real women who admired these films" (169), but was also herself "the last of the independent actress/ producer holdouts from the silent era" (187). In *Mulholland Drive*, Betty Elms is Diane's oneiric fantasy of herself free of the cruelty that surrounds her in her waking life. But these two films, both extremely dark in their suggestion of a brutal disregard for human need, desire, and creativity, suggest an alternative in the imaginative sympathy they invite for their heroines—Betty's gorgeous audition; Norma's Chaplin impression, her physical and verbal grand gestures.

In *Sunset Boulevard*, Cecil B. DeMille offers sympathy for Norma's plight, but the tone of his compassion is paternalistic; he insists to his assistant that Paramount abandon its only real interest in Norma, leasing her antique car, an Isotta-Fraschini—"Never mind the car—I'll buy him a thousand cars." Such patriarchal kindness extended to Norma can be contrasted with Joe's final voice-over commentary, which extends sympathy for Norma that resonates both because of its helplessness (Joe is dead) and its acuity in lambasting the opportunistic institutional forces of the Hollywood celebrity machine and the police:

> [T]he whole joint was jumping—cops, reporters, neighbors, passersby, as much hoopdedoo as we get in Los Angeles when they open a Super Market. Even the newsreel guys came roaring in [ironically, from Paramount Pictures News Division]. Here was an item everybody could have some fun with. The heartless so-and-sos!

What would they do to Norma? Even if she got away with it in court—crime of passion, temporary insanity— those headlines would kill her: "Forgotten Star a Slayer," "Aging Actress," "Yesterday's Glamour Queen."

The "femme fatale" idea is evoked throughout the film, suggested below in Norma's menacing final spider grab at the viewer. Nevertheless the figure of the "femme fatale" is contextualized in a strongly sympathetic portrait of Norma's tragedy and the forces that process and dispose of her as an image.

At the end, she's lost in madness, but the madness is mediated by our appreciation of the performance: "those reels were turning after all," says Joe's voice-over. Just as the woman in Gilman's "The Yellow Wallpaper" escapes her gendered prison into madness, so too does Norma Desmond, but the film ends with mercy, in a tribute to her, Norma Desmond controlling the camera's and our gaze (Figure 5.2).
Joe's sympathy is only possible from the perspective of death, Joe no longer having anything to lose. His posthumous sympathy extends a challenge to viewers, I think, to let go of our need for control and projection and to respond with emotional and intellectual depth

Figure 5.2 "I'm ready for my close-up." Norma Desmond (Gloria Swanson) in *Sunset Boulevard* (1950) © Paramount Pictures. All rights reserved. Courtesy of Paramount Pictures. BFI.

to vital moments, exercising what poet John Keats called negative capability, an empathy propelled by images and language. Lynch interestingly links empathy and intuitive knowing not to "femininity," but to the detective mode, helping us to understand his rewriting of noir as a feminist call for engagement:

> I think that intuition—the detective in us—puts things together in a way that makes sense for us. They say intuition gives you an inner knowing, but the weird thing about inner knowing is that it's really hard to communicate that to someone else.
>
> (288)

While Lynch himself says that poets do this in words, clearly his investment is in trying to adumbrate a filmic rendering of such "knowing," a drawing forth of viewers who, in Lynch's words, "feel-think" responses to film. As Douglas says in the frame narrative of Henry James's *The Turn of the Screw* (1898): "The story won't tell . . . not in any literal vulgar way" (3). Like the literary modernists, Lynch seeks to establish new grounds on which individuals connect and communicate, bridging traumatic psychological and social gaps with rich moments of human connection or meaningful insight.

In this, Lynch resembles not only James but also Virginia Woolf. In *Mrs Dalloway* (1925), Virginia Woolf explores modern alienation—in Septimus Smith's shell shock, ("human nature, in short, was on him" [92]); in Lucrezia's loss in having been uprooted from her pastoral female world in Italy; and in Clarissa's struggle for connection and independence within the terms of convention, patriarchy, and mortality. Against these battles, however, there are indeed moments that affirm human vitality, imagination, and empathy—in Clarissa's observation of her neighbor, the old woman she sees moving about through the window: "here was one room; there another. Did religion solve that, or love?" (127). As in *Mrs Dalloway*—in, for example, Clarissa's kiss with Sally Seton, "the most exquisite moment of her whole life" (35)—in *Mulholland Drive*, discrete moments of human connection are the salve to trauma and alienation. That is why Lynch emphasizes seemingly obscure moments of connection, epiphanic moments that extend beyond their narrative purview, such as the locked gaze between Adam Kesher and Betty, when Betty follows the casting agent to audition for the part she "would kill—." In this Jamesian moment of recognition, Kesher seems to intuitively turn around in his seat, in the middle of auditioning singers. When he turns, the camera first moves in to show him looking at Betty, then cuts to a reverse shot, as the camera zooms in to show Betty returning Adam's gaze. Adam recognizes Betty somehow ("This is the girl"?), and Betty recognizes Adam's subjectivity, when we've been inclined to read him as both smug and a dupe. This moment suggests flexibility in reading Adam sympathetically, which Diane's dream adumbrates here.

Nochimson focuses in her analysis of this scene on its evocation of the Hollywood cliché of the discovered young actress: "the director is struck immediately by an unknown girl," recalling Lloyd Bacon's 1933 *42nd St.* For Nochimson, the cliché is invoked here to point to failure, since "the moment of inspiration does not take place" (Sheen and Davison, 172), and Betty's talent never bears fruit. While Nochimson's observation is interesting, I think the "shock of authentic contact" between Adam and Betty (Nochimson, *Film Quarterly*, 41) is more a register of their bond and shared recognition of a yearning for connection and meaningful expression—the scene, in other words, is more about what's possible, rather than what isn't (Betty's being discovered).

There are two other central scenes in the film that reach beyond their narrative limits, both connected to the loss of Betty. The first is the memorable performance by Rebekah del Rio at the Club Silencio. The lip-synching that is revealed, after del Rio drops to the ground and the singing continues, suggests, as the Club sequence does more generally, Lynch's interest in imagining a transcendence of logical narrative sense. The scene revels in illusion, in a self-conscious undoing of cinematic expectation. What is most striking about del Rio's brilliant rendering of Roy Orbison's "Crying" in Spanish is its contextless emotional register, accentuated in the a capella delivery. Beyond the general theme of loss that the song evokes (the loss of Betty and her optimism, the loss of the love and passion between Betty and Rita), its effect is more than the sum of its thematic parts. Hudson says it forges a new "language," one that "communicates that which is intensely felt but cannot be manifested in words" (23). Hudson is right here, but the brilliance of the scene is that it is powerful both as an aesthetic experience and as a commentary on the loss and desire that the film enacts. The song is a modernist wail. Cast in del Rio's beautiful voice, "Crying" attaches to no one and everyone and marries universal cries of loneliness and unmet desire to art and illusion, to the music and blue setting (blue, as Andrews says, "the color of guilt, madness, and death") and multilevel performances that satisfy for only the moment the need for consolation. The scene demonstrates Lynch's remarkable ability to draw us deeply into an affective moment of transcendence and passionate human connection through artistic expression at the same time as we are profoundly aware of the inevitability of the moment's end: thus the trauma and tears of Betty and Rita, especially Betty, who shakes visibly as she sits in the audience, presumably because her very identity is defined by Diane's own moment of imaginative dream-expression.

The other moment in the film that reaches beyond its narrative limits but that is key to the film's purpose is the one in which Camilla guides Diane through a "short cut" up the hill to the party that will cement the jealous desperation that moves Diane to have Camilla killed. Camilla's guiding of Diane up through the woods contrasts sharply with the register of all of Camilla's and Diane's scenes. Lynch holds the sadomasochistic nature of these women's relationship in abeyance, as he shifts the tone of the scene, reorienting us back from Diane's cynicism to the Rita/Betty dream sequence, just for an extended moment. The walk through the woods tonally harkens back to Rita and Betty's trusting bond because their physical ascent here and the mystery of the setting—"the secret path," as Camilla labels it—recalls their dream adventure (which has already taken place in the film but has not yet been imagined by Diane). As in the dream sequence starring Betty and Rita, here, Diane and Camilla look at each other lovingly, with an openness that evokes great poignance surrounding the loss of Betty. In this moment, Betty's openness, vitality, and hopefulness replace angry and desperate Diane, as Naomi Watts's affect transforms again from the bitterness we see in Diane's gait, demeanor, and facial expressions to the warm, friendly, and receptive manner of Betty. On the one hand, the scene draws forth iconic noir female figures, as it did earlier when Rita and Betty walked through the courtyard toward Diane's apartment—and, indeed, throughout the film in Lynch's many two-shots of, first, the blonde Betty and dark-haired Rita, then, as the film inches toward a discovery of their both being part of Diane Selwyn's imagination, the blonde Betty and the blonde Rita. On the other hand, however, here, the discrete iconic figures melt away into a moment in which Betty and Rita merge with Diane and Camilla, and Lynch invokes a tone of entreatment and of loving connection. That the film in this moment makes us mourn the loss of Betty suggests its hopefulness and belief. We are able to imaginatively project Betty onto Diane in a gesture of empathy and the power of the image and the filmic moment to transcend narrative logic. As Nochimson says of *Mulholland Drive*, "it is only the larger faculty [of imagination] that can apprehend what is really going on, a truth too absurd for ordinary logic and reason" (Sheen and Davison, 170).

Filmic moments have the extraordinary power to evoke other moments, past and future. As Lynch himself says:

> There are all kinds of opportunities to re-live the past and there are new things coming up every second. There is some kind of present, but the present is the most elusive because it's going real fast.
>
> (278)

The walk together up the wooded hill is the closest to a "return," in Norma Desmond's terms, the actress will have in *Mulholland Drive*, and it's a scene that gains its power from affect, a modernist moment of identification with the loss of Diane's hopes and the loss of the image of that very hopefulness in Betty Elms. The scene evokes the power of the past in the present.

In narrative terms, of course, neither Diane Selwyn nor Norma Desmond will have a "return," although ironically, the day after Peg Entwistle committed suicide in 1932 by climbing then jumping off the "Hollywood" "H," she is said to have been offered a leading role in a play about a woman driven to suicide. In *Sunset Boulevard*, the kindly patriarch DeMille lets Norma maintain her fantasy, but when her gigolo boyfriend Joe Gilles leaves her (she thinks, for his young pretty untainted scriptwriter Betty Schaefer), she shoots him in the back and loses her touch with reality completely.

Significantly, in one among many detachments from "reality" in *Mulholland Drive*, Rita names herself after a poster of Rita Hayworth as Gilda, the epitome of a woman branded by audiences' insistence that she is a "femme fatale." In fact, as those who have carefully watched the movie know, and as I've discussed in earlier chapters, Gilda is more victimized by Johnny's misogyny than she is a victimizer (a fatal woman). Lynch suggests the idea of "femme fatale" as illusion in *Mulholland Drive*, as Laura Harring's amnesiac character scans the bathroom of Betty's aunt's apartment, looking in panic to name herself. Her gaze falls on the *Gilda* poster, on which the film's tagline reads, "There never was a woman like Gilda." The repetition of the simile "a woman like . . .," as in "a woman like Ann" Sutton, or Devlin's mistrust (where I began this book) that "a woman like [Alicia] could ever change her spots," suggests an abiding instability in men's belief in women, a gravitational pull toward the comfortable stance of simile and the cultural hazards of gender metaphors and generalization. Lynch literalizes the promotion line—there never was indeed "a woman like Gilda"—cutting to a shot of the poster reflected in the cosmetic magnifying glass and underscoring the idea of the "femme fatale" as image, as a dream reflection of the desires of those seeking control or seeking, to various degrees of investment and force, to solidify control or maintain invulnerability.

When Rita tells Betty, "I don't know who I am," Betty's response is funny—"You're Rita." But her affirmation of the fiction also indicates the status of identity markers in film, notably the "femme fatale," as utterly constructed and the result of projected illusion. In "fact," Rita is Diane's projection, just as Betty is.

***

As interested in dreams as *Mulholland Drive* obviously is, I think, in fact, that the lesson of the film is not to get lost in illusion and dreams. We have to keep our wits about us; we need to keep alternate realities in our minds simultaneously, remaining critical and engaged viewers of images that can tap into our desires, not just as psychosexual subjects, as much feminist film theory has demonstrated, but also as purveyors of cultural ideation about female agency and power. Such flexibility in our response to representation requires empathy and imagination. In larger terms, we need to be a little more invested in agency rather than power; activity rather than influence; creativity rather than control. These values model a more sustainable feminism for women and men and, I believe, promise a more meaningful experience of art and more productive conversations about our cultural habits than we're generally able to arrive at.

Notes

Introduction   "No One Mourns the Wicked"

1. "But a reduction in the female image has taken place, for by definition the *femme fatale* is a stereotype designating the mysterious and unknowable power of women, whereas the role of prostitute represents a more defined sexual role, amenable to social control, and shorn of the earlier stereotype's fatality. . . . [Bree Daniel's] changeability is no longer part of the grand manner of the *femme fatale*, it is simply neurotic. Her changes in mood are not incomprehensible, but motivated by a consistent psychology explained as a response to the alienating demands of modern society" (Gledhill, 1978, 122).
2. I think here of Susan Knobloch's discussion of Sharon Stone's star text as violent woman: "The plots of her films . . . lean hard upon the contemporary notion that male violence toward women and women's families provokes and sometimes justifies female violence" (126).
3. While Kaplan suggests in her new edition of *Women in Film Noir* that there is no longer dispute concerning the idea that "meaning about woman is produced through the work of a film" (3) (she quotes Christine Gledhill's excellent point that "ideological myths about women are as much a part of the real world as any other construct"), I believe that there are still serious demands made on popular representation to portray women in terms of role modeling. I have written on this issue in connection with Todd Haynes's remarkable film *Safe*, a deeply feminist film about environmental illness that suggests, without at all "heroicizing" its female protagonist Carol White (Julianne Moore), a brutal relationship between female agency, female victimization, and social institutions. See Julie Grossman, "The Trouble with Carol: The Costs of Feeling Good in Todd Haynes's [*Safe*] and the American Cultural Landscape."
4. In her essay "Is the Gaze Male," E. Ann Kaplan quotes Karen Horney's 1932 article, "The Dread of Woman," which helps to explain (and resonates in the context of) the overdetermined anti-Hillary venom: "Men have never tired of fashioning expressions for the violent force by which man feels himself drawn to the woman, and side by side with his longing, the dread that through her he might die and be undone" (280). While many of the women writers musing on the meaning of Hillary Clinton in the anthology *Thirty Ways of Looking at Hillary* (2008) are sympathetic to Clinton, such a project itself institutionalizes the practice of appropriating Clinton's image and mythifying the woman at the cost of examining her public policies and whether or not she would be an effective president.
5. Susan Bordo comments on the absurd aftermath of the cookie incident, characterized by popular distress at Clinton's perceived contempt for domestic values:

> Rightly protesting this interpretation, Hillary Clinton tried to prove her womanhood by producing her favorite recipe for oatmeal chocolate chip cookies. Barbara Bush, apparently feeling that a gauntlet had been thrown

down, responded in kind with a richer, less fibre-conscious recipe of her own. Newspapers across the country asked readers to prepare both and vote on which First Lady had the better cookie.

(122)

6. I'd like to thank John Cant from the University of Essex for calling my attention to this image at the "Cinematicity" Conference in Essex in the spring of 2007.
7. Said Tomasky, "Once again, it's all about Hillary Clinton, who delivered the most abrasive, self-absorbed, selfish, delusional, emasculating and extortionate political speech I've heard in a long time. And I've left out some adjectives, just to be polite" (guardian.co.uk, June 5, 2008).
8. Hoyt reports that Dowd, along with another *New York Times* columnist, William Kristol, was inducted into the National Organization for Women's Media "Hall of Shame," initiated at the conclusion of Hillary Clinton's primary campaign for the presidency.

1   Film Noir's "Femmes Fatales": Moving Beyond Gender Fantasies

1. I am indebted to Phillip Novak for his insight concerning Cora's victimization and the particular oppressiveness of her environment that this scene reveals.
2. I therefore disagree with Foster Hirch's designation of the film as "deeply conservative": "Kelly must be punished. A deeply conservative 1950s morality underwrites Fuller's pulp poetry: to maintain a 'civilized environment,' the femme fatale cannot be redeemed and must be expelled alone into a moral wilderness" (*Detours and Lost Highways*, 194). As Fuller's comment above, as well as the logic of the narrative, suggests, the film expresses sympathy for Kelly's victimization by the hypocritical townspeople.
3. See Phillip Novak's elegant commentary on Jake's misreading in "The *Chinatown* Syndrome," which appeared in the Summer, 2007 issue of *Criticism*.
4. Leslie Fiedler comments on a similar dynamic in literary representation of women:

> There are not, in fact, two orders of women, good and bad, nor is there even one which seems for a little while bad, only to prove in the end utterly unravished and pure. There are only two sets of expectations and a single imperfect kind of woman caught between them: only actual incomplete females, looking in vain for a satisfactory definition of their role in a land of artists who insist on treating them as goddesses or bitches. The dream role and the nightmare role alike deny the humanity of women, who, baffled, switch from playing out one to acting out the other.
>
> (314)

5. Although Oliver and Trigo get the names wrong in their commentary on *Out of the Past*—Jim [Richard Webb] is not Jeff's deaf–mute assistant; he's the

upright Bridgeport petty tyrant in love with Ann—their comments on Ann are intriguing in the context of broadening our preconceived notions of the kinds of roles played by women in noir: "Ann Miller is a proto-'femme fatale,' displaying the same curiosity, the same desire, and the same willingness to travel to all the exotic places where the noir hero is headed or from where he has returned" (224).

6. The scene recalls earlier noir protagonists committing violence to protect a set of ideas about gender and innocence and to express pent-up frustration about failed masculinity. After stabbing Kitty March in *Scarlet Street* (1945), Chris Cross projects his anger onto Johnny, denying any responsibility for his own actions: "You [meaning Kitty] were innocent, you were pure! That's what he killed in you! He's the murderer!"

7. When I invoke here noir's "gray view of the world," I understand the interest shown by Thom Anderson and others in describing the polemics and pessimism of *film gris*. The category calls attention to the leftist politics of filmmakers such as Abraham Polonsky and Jules Dassin (both blacklisted by the HUAC), whose work speaks to the desire of filmmakers to subvert the mainstream ameliorative Hollywood formula. Such generic boundaries are, however, hard again to maintain. The gray view of the world is, I think, more systematically present in film noir than the classification of *film gris* implies. If *film gris* is, for example, defined as "Social critique [that] focuses on the critique of the law as a boundary dividing society into a good, legal world and a bad, illegal world" (Joshua Hirsch, 85), such critique is surely present, as many of my allusions to film noir throughout this book suggest, in many movies categorized more widely as film noir.

8. Mulvey (1989) reconsidered and revised her position here, notably in "Afterthoughts on Visual Pleasure and Narrative Cinema," in which she considered the power and pitfalls of the female spectator, the latter having to do with "the female spectator's fantasy of masculinisation at cross-purposes with itself" (37).

9. An example of the effects of genre conception on how we draw connections among films and texts can be seen in Maria DiBattista's analysis of the "fast-talking dame" in her book of the same title. DiBattista captures the strength and vitality of the smart verbal women in Hollywood comedies of the 1930s and 1940s. Female characters played by smart vibrant actresses such as Carole Lombard, Rosiland Russell, Katherine Hepburn, Claudette Colbert, and Barbara Stanwyck illustrate for viewers something very positive in the films in which they starred, in part because the generic demands of comedy make it possible for the women in these films to model something very positive for viewers: that smart ambitious women can find happiness in social and private worlds. These women are subversive, causing chaos, just as film noir's women often do, however, and DiBattista's description of the upheaval caused by fast-talking dames in the films of Preston Sturges might well describe the anxieties represented in film noir about female dissembling:

> His comedies show us what transpires when men find themselves fallen into a world—or a love—that does not conform to their notions of physical and moral order. Men often enter this world without suitable

guides, and often without sufficient guile. Guile is an intellectual vice conventionally ascribed to woman, the conniving Eve. Comedy, in its iconoclastic moods, interprets this vice as a virtue and the designing woman our beset, if unconventional, teacher.

(306)

It is often noted that noir women have "guile," but the emphasis is much more on this than on the fact that, like DiBattista's fast-talking dames in Hollywood's comedies, film noir's modern women of the same period have something to teach us about the chaos that is perceived when gender roles shift within society. Such insight can be hindered by strict adherence to the premises of genre.

10. Cowie explains:

The connection between *film noir* and melodrama has been made by a number of writers, but usually in order to distinguish *film noir* as a form of male melodrama, in contrast to the woman's film and female melodrama. Maureen Turin, for example, points out that "*noir* and the woman's film are two sides of the same coin in Hollywood's forties symbolic circulation." Murray Smith suggests that the investigation of the woman in *film noir* is mirrored in the female gothic melodrama's investigation of the man. Frank Krutnik also argues in terms of parallel genres:
The "tough" thrillers tend to treat the drama of their "dislocated" heroes seriously. . . . Just as the dramatic representation of the realm of women—issues of the family, home, romance, motherhood, female identity and desire—have been approached . . . in terms of the generic category of the "woman's picture melodrama," one could consider the "tough" thriller as representing a form of "masculine melodrama" (krutnik).

(Cowie, 129–30)

Cowie is drawing here from Turin's "Flashbacks and the Psyche in Melodrama and Film Noir" (182), Murray Smith's "*Film Noir* and the Female Gothic and *Deception*" (64), and Krutnik's *In a Lonely Street* (164).

Many feminist readers of film noir have expressed the concern that critical emphasis should shift away from the male as the source of narrative and interest in noir. Such focus on male behavior (men's postwar anxiety, confusion, and post-traumatic shock—"the maladjusted males," says Thomas Schatz, "whose alienation and anxiety clearly invoked the general postwar climate" [4–5]) foregrounds sympathy for the motives and sufferings of these male characters, concealing female subjectivity as well as the offenses to women represented in these films. Susan Hayward, for example, worries about "male-centered" noir, concern expressed in her closing remarks at the "Cherchez la Femme" conference held at Exeter in September of 2005, organized by Helen Hanson and Catherine O'Rawe. Hayward's references to the co-opting of representations of female power by men echoes concerns Tania Modleski voiced in 1991 in *Feminism Without Women*, in which Modleski explored the extent to which feminism(s) has (have) been appropriated by men, deactivating the political force of feminism through the anodyne language of equality supported by gender studies.

2 "Well, aren't we ambitious": Desire, Domesticity, and the "Femme Fatale," or "You've made up your mind I'm guilty": The Long Reach of Misreadings of Woman as Wicked in American Film Noir

1. "*Gilda* argues that images of charismatic female sexuality generally provoke this kind of ambivalence in men, and goes on to suggest that in such cases heterosexual feeling is accompanied by feelings of impotence and inferiority which can only be made good by overpowering, degrading and—logically— destroying the woman" (Britton, 220).
2. In *Impact* (1949), sex and gender anxiety is again conflated with American business and capitalism, as Walt Williams (Brian Donlevy) is introduced to us as a master businessman whose first gesture in the film is to change the mind of the entire board of directors of his company about a major acquisition. Walter's masculinity is linked to his mastery and ownership, as is exemplified when he explains to his wife that he likes monograms because they reflect that things "belong to me." This exchange introduces the motif of threatened impotence, as Walt admits to his wife that he has "only one vulnerable spot," meaning her. She calls him "Softy," a name that takes on echoic resonance later, when Walt realizes that his wife has been cheating on him and planned to kill him with her lover Jim. In the first moments of Walt's realization, he hears "Softy" over and over in his mind, reminiscent for noir viewers of Kitty and Johnny's haunting of Chris Cross's fevered imagination at the end of *Scarlet Street*. In both films, a sexual, psychological, and social loss of power is figured in a male protagonist becoming emasculated by a woman and her lover. In both films, money and capital function as the dominant context for defining the desires of these duped men.
3. Examples, as I suggested in Chapter 1, abound in film noir: Scotty in discovering "Madeleine" is Judy in *Vertigo*; Johnny, in discovering that Joyce Harwood is married to Eddie in *The Blue Dahlia*; Travis Bickle, spurned by the initially "angelic" Betsy to finally insist that she'll "burn in hell like the rest of them" in *Taxi Driver*.

3 Psychological Disorders and "Wiretapping the Unconscious": Film Noir Listens to Women

1. Says Snyder, "[t]he Antisocial Personality Disorder is characterized by a disregard for, and violation of, the rights of others. Its traits include unlawful behavior, deceitfulness, impulsivity, irritability, aggressiveness, reckless disregard for the safety of self or others, irresponsibility, and lack of remorse. The Borderline Personality Disorder is defined by instability in interpersonal relationships, self-image, and affects as well as marked impulsivity. Identity disturbance, suicide attempts or self-mutilation, difficulty in modulating oftentimes intense, inappropriate anger, and chronic feelings of emptiness are frequent. A pattern of excessive emotionality and attention seeking is seen in the Histrionic Personality Disorder. Sexually provocative behavior, shallow expressions of emotion, self-dramatization and theatricality, suggestibility,

and superficial interpersonal relationships are core features. Grandiosity, a need for admiration, and a lack of empathy distinguish the Narcissistic Personality Disorder. Individuals with this disorder believe they are 'special,' have a sense of entitlement, exploit others, and manifest envy, arrogance, and haughtiness. These four personality disorders comprise what the DSM-IV refers to as 'Cluster B' personality disorders" (157).

2. Then, too, Peter William Evans has argued that even Phyllis, quintessential "femme fatale," can be seen as the victim of patriarchal oppression, as her husband is an alcoholic brute and Neff infantalizes her, calling her "baby" and assuming control of their murder plan.

3. See Gluck: "By 1944, when war production was beginning to wind down, and especially in 1945, when the end of the war was in sight, the attitudes toward women workers underwent an about-face. Where earlier the working mother with her child-care problems had been the object of commiseration, she became now the object of blame for the rising rate of juvenile delinquency. Where the young factory worker had been portrayed as directly contributing to the war effort through her labor, she came to be treated primarily as a decorative object that would inspire fighting men to greater and better feats. The *Lockheed Star*, for example, had regularly run stories about their women production workers. In mid-1944, these were supplanted by cheesecake photo contests. Furthermore, there were fewer and fewer photos of women factory workers and more and more of office workers. Clearly, women production workers were being phased out—if not in actuality, then certainly in the public consciousness. Preparations were being made for the postwar world" (15).

4. It would be interesting to wonder about *Scarlet Street*'s Kitty March in the context of pathology and invalidation. Kitty's masochistic and desperate drive to be with the brutal Johnny "Prince" can be read as a perverse attempt to elicit validation. She says about Chris Cross (versus Johnny), "[i]f he were mean or vicious or if he'd bawl me out or something, I'd like him better." That her masochism in the film, submitting to Johnny's exploitation of her as a tool to extract money from Chris Cross, is linked to invalidation may be supported by the narrative interest in Kitty's becoming validated and recognized as a talented artist by the art critic Janeway.

4   Looking Back—*Victorinoir*: Modern Women and the Fatal(e) Progeny of Victorian Representations

1. In Coventry Patmore's "The Angel in the House" (Ricks, 321–2), the speaker's "sadness [is] banish'd far" by the workings of the domestic female angel. This poem became increasingly popular after its initial publication in 1854. Martha Vicinus has noted the high stakes of maintaining the angel's prominent role: "Rigid social rules ensured the safety of the bourgeois family; within the home, women were assigned a special position as caretakers of morality and religion, for their unique sensibility made them alone capable of child care and domestic responsibilities" (2).

2. The virtue of compromise (and accommodation) is hailed throughout Victorian fiction. In the face of the hard rigors of "the real," Pip eventually compromises his "great expectations"; Rochester, in the end a "caged eagle" (439), sacrifices

his "will" and passion to live "happily" in an isolated forest dwelling with Jane. In *Far from the Madding Crowd*, Bathsheba progresses from her rash and undisciplined romance with Troy to settle with the sturdy Gabriel Oak. Isabel Archer accepts the limits of her desires in mature recognition of the failure of her marriage to Gilbert; Hareton and Cathy Linton take up "normal" domestic life, shorn of the passion and chaotic desire that characterized the relationship between Heathcliff and Catherine; and finally, in a wistful but bracing allusion to past models of heroic action (past venues, I should add, defined by myths of force and mastery), George Eliot says the following: "the medium in which their ardent deeds took shape is for ever gone" (*Middlemarch*, 766).

3. In "From 'Passionate Attachments' to Dis-Identification," Žižek attempts to recover the contemporary (postmodern) "femme fatale" because of the way she "brutally [destroys] the spectral aura of 'feminine mystery,' by acting as a cold manipulating subject interested only in raw sex." Žižek interestingly contends that the new "femme fatale"'s "strategy is the one of deceiving the male protagonist by openly telling the truth. The male partner is unable to accept this, and so, he desperately clings to the conviction that, behind the cold manipulative surface, there must be a heart of gold to be saved, a person of warm human feeling" (para 10). As my reading of Kathy Moffett and women in noir generally suggests, this pattern is already present in original-cycle film noir. Something similar is happening, as I suggested in Chapter 1, in Travis Bickle's obsession with Iris's "heart of gold" in *Taxi Driver*.

4. In her intriguing essay about Sheridan Le Fanu's *Carmilla* (1872), Tamar Heller writes about the female vampire's expression of nineteenth-century cultural anxiety about female desire. Heller discusses how female desire is interpreted by medical discourse as hysterical, as in the theories of Weir Mitchell I alluded to in Chapter 3 (that figured so prominently in Gilman's "The Yellow Wallpaper"). The "appetite" of Le Fanu's vampire is particularly transgressive insofar as Carmilla is linked sexually to Laura:

> [S]ince female homoeroticism excludes men and eludes control, to figure female sexuality as lesbianism underscores the threat that women's desire poses to male authority—a threat that would become increasingly pronounced in the decades to follow Le Fanu's story, as feminist agitation further politicized bonds between women.
>
> (79)

5. The idea of scapegoating unconventional women to maintain purity and clearly demarcated gender boundaries has cultural resonance in contemporary popular culture, in, for example, the broad success of the novel and stage musical *Wicked*. The novel by Gregory Maguire, *Wicked: The Life and Times of the Wicked Witch of the West*, reimagines the iconic moral poles of *The Wizard of Oz*, as does the book *Wicked* by Winnie Holzman, brought to life on stage first in 2003 with music and lyrics by Stephen Schwartz. *Wicked* (which became a touchstone for "Ugly Betty" in the television series of the same name) addresses the cultural habit of scapegoating to unify the population—"something bad is happening in Oz."

6. "Carmilla's execution suggests a feminized version of castration; moreover, the stake driven through the body of the lesbian vampire whose biting had mimicked

the act of penetration is a raw assertion of phallic power. Yet, in the light of the tale's thematics of female knowledge, it is also telling that Carmilla is decapitated, and that her head, site of knowledge and of voice, is struck off" (Heller, 90).

7. Recall Dave Bannion at the auto yard in *The Big Heat* and Guy Haines talking (in *Strangers on a Train*) from behind the grate, symbolically taking on Bruno's criminality after Bruno tells him he has killed Guy's wife.

5   Looking Forward: Deconstructing The "Femme Fatale"

1. See Tom Gunning's superb analysis in *The Films of Fritz Lang: Allegories of Vision and Modernity* (2000) of Lang's "master criminals" and the many men in his films obsessed with having or maintaining control. Mabuse (like Mr. Roque, as Chion notes) "stands as the archetypal Langian figure who attempts to maintain control of the film's narrative action and the processes of the Destiny-machine by becoming the master criminal organizer, the energy at the center of the technological web" (Gunning, 100).

2. The female detective figure, the setting of Hollywood as a dream factory, and the noir generic trappings were recently combined in the film adaptation of *Nancy Drew: The Mystery in Hollywood Hills*, with young Emma Roberts as the earnest young detective and also featuring *Mulholland Drive's* Laura Harring. The appropriation of Nancy Drew by film noir exemplifies a strange acculturation into the values of binary opposition, for example, by way of a Level-2 "Easy to Read" book, *Nancy Drew: Hello, Hollywood* by Fern Alexander, made available in 2007 by Simon and Shuster's Children's Publishing Division, to five to seven-year-old girls: "Nancy could not believe her eyes when they arrived in Los Angeles. The city was so busy and noisy! It was a big change from River Heights" (5), then a few pages later, "At lunch, [Nancy] sat next to Trish in the cafeteria. Trish laughed when Nancy laid out her napkin with chicken-salad sandwiches, carrot sticks, apple slices, a cupcake, and hot cocoa. Nancy was definitely not from LA!" (11). The book demonstrates schematically not only the city/country dichotomy (again the "River" in the hometown name denoting naturalness vs. the artificiality and danger of the big city), but also constructs a severe break between innocent good girls ("With her cardigan, handbag, and spiral-bound notebook, Nancy looked really out of place!" [9]) and experienced bad girls; the Hollywood High "mean girls" have irony and play tricks on Nancy. These oppositions are presented without analysis, change, or insight and are, in the end, affirmed: "Hollywood had been an adventure. . . . But [Nancy] really looked forward to returning to her friends—especially Ned!" (32).

3. Hudson understands Rita's "not having a fixed sense" in relation to Kristeva's "chora," the "sujet en process (subject in process)" that represents a "blurring of conceptual borders" (23) and that "[disrupts] the process of signification" (19). Hudson's application of post-structuralist psychoanalysis catches much of the spirit of the film but stops short, with its investment in Lynch's aesthetics, of registering the full significance of the "fluidity and promise that comes from not having a fixed self" (20).

Works Cited

Alexander, Fern. *Nancy Drew: Hello, Hollywood*. New York: Simon and Schuster, 2007.

Anderson, Thom. "Red Hollywood," *Literature and the Visual Arts in Contemporary Society*. Ed. Suzanne Ferguson and Barbara S. Groseclose. Columbus, OH: Ohio State University Press, 1985. 141–96.

Andrews, David. "An Oneiric Fugue: The Various Logics of Mulholland Drive," *Journal of Film and Video* 56.1 (2004). 25–40.

Ardis, Ann. *New Women, New Novels: Feminism and Early Modernism*. New Brunswick, NJ: Rutgers University Press, 1990.

Bacall, Lauren. *Lauren Bacall by Myself*. Book club (ed.). New York: Knopf, 1978.

Barefoot, Guy. *Gaslight Melodrama: From Victorian London to 1940s Hollywood*. London; New York: Continuum, 2001.

Biesen, Sheri Chinen. *Blackout: World War II and the Origins of Film Noir*. Baltimore: Johns Hopkins University Press, 2005.

"Bleak House" (review). *The Bioscope*, February 26, 1920. 56.

Bordo, Susan. *Unbearable Weight: Feminism, Western Culture, and the Body*. Berkeley: University of California Press, 1993.

Britton, Andrew. "Betrayed by Rita Hayworth: Misogyny in *The Lady from Shanghai*," *The Book of Film Noir*. Ed. Ian Cameron. New York: Continuum, 1993. 213–21.

Bronfen, Elisabeth. "Femme Fatale: Negotiations of Tragic Desire," *New Literary History* 35.1 (2004). 103–16.

Brontë, Emily. *Wuthering Heights*. Ed. Linda Peterson. New York: Bedford Books, 1992.

Brontë, Charlotte. *Jane Eyre*. Harmondsworth, Middlesex, England; New York, NY: Penguin, 1997.

Buckler, William Earl and Thomas Hardy. *The Poetry of Thomas Hardy: A Study in Art and Ideas*. New York: New York University Press, 1983.

Buszek, Maria Elena. *Pin-Up Grrrls: Feminism, Sexuality, Popular Culture*. Durham, NC: Duke University Press, 2006.

Cain, James M. *The Postman Always Rings Twice*. 1st Vintage crime/Black Lizard ed. New York: Vintage Books, 1992.

Cameron, Ian Alexander. *The Book of Film Noir*. New York: Continuum, 1993.

Card, James. *Seductive Cinema: The Art of Silent Film*. 1st ed. New York: Knopf, 1994.

Chandler, Raymond and Frank MacShane. *Later Novels and Other Writings*. Vol. 80. New York: Library of America, 1995.

Chion, Michael. *David Lynch*. Trans. Robert Julian. 2nd ed. London: British Film Institute, 2006.

Conrad, Joseph. *Heart of Darkness and The Secret Sharer*. New York: Signet Classic, 1997.

Copjec, Joan (ed.). *Shades of Noir: A Reader*. London; New York: Verso, 1993.

Cowie, Elizabeth. "*Film Noir* and Women," *Shades of Noir*. Ed. Joan Copjec. New York: Verso, 1993. 121–66.

Dargis, Manohla. "Review of *The Star Machine* by Jeanne Basinger," *The New York Times*, December 30, 2007, sec. Book Review: 17.

———. "Review of *There Will Be Blood*," *The New York Times*, December 26, 2007, sec. Arts and Leisure: 1.

Davidson, David. "From Virgin to Dynamo: The 'Amoral Woman' in European Cinema," *Cinema Journal* 21.1 (Fall 1981). 31–58.

De Beauvoir, Simone. "From *Brigitte Bardot and the Lolita Syndrome*," *Women and the Cinema: A Critical Anthology*. Ed. Karyn Kay and Gerald Peary. New York: E. P. Dutton, 1977. 112–16.

Deslippe, Dennis A. *"Rights, Not Roses": Unions and the Rise of Working-Class Feminism, 1945–1980*. Urbana and Chicago: University of Illinois Press, 2000.

DiBattista, Maria. *Fast-Talking Dames*. New Haven and London: Yale University Press, 2001.

Dickens, Charles. *Bleak House*. Harmondsworth: Penguin, 1971.

———. *Great Expectations*. London, New York: Penguin Books, 1965.

Dijkstra, Bram. *Idols of Perversity: Fantasies of Feminine Evil in Fin-De-Siècle Culture*. New York: Oxford University Press, 1986.

Dirks, Tim. "The Postman Always Rings Twice," *American Movie Channel*. <http://www.filmsite.org/post.html>. Accessed on May 29, 2009.

Doane, Mary Ann. "The Clinical Eye: Medical Discourses in the 'Woman's Film' of the 1940s," *Poetics Today* 6.1/2. 205–27.

———. *Femmes Fatales: Feminism, Film Theory, and Psychoanalysis*. New York: Routledge, 1991.

Dyer, Richard. "Resistance Through Charisma: Rita Hayworth and *Gilda*," *Women in Film Noir*. Ed. E. Ann Kaplan. London: British Film Institute, 1998. 115–22.

———. "Lana: Four Films of Lana Turner," *Imitation of Life: A Reader on Film and Television Melodrama*. Ed. Marcia Landy. Wayne State University Press, 1991. 409–28.

Eliot, George. *The Mill on the Floss*. Oxford: Oxford University Press, 1981.

———. *Middlemarch*. New York: Bantam, 1985.

Elsaesser, Thomas. "Lulu and the Meter Man: Louise Brooks, Pabst, and 'Pandora's Box,'" *Screen* 24.4–5 (1983). 4–36.

Erens, Patricia. *Issues in Feminist Film Criticism*. Bloomington: Indiana University Press, 1990.

Evans, Peter Willliam. "Double Indemnity (Or Bringing Up Baby)," *The Book of Film Noir*. Ed. Ian Cameron. New York: Continuum, 1993. 165–73.

Ferguson, Suzanne and Barbara S. Groseclose. *Literature and the Visual Arts in Contemporary Society*. Columbus: Ohio State University Press, 1985.

Fiedler, Leslie A. *Love and Death in the American Novel*. New York: Criterion Books, 1960.

Fisher, Ian. "Grisly Murder Case Intrigues Italian University City," *The New York Times*, November 13, 2007.

Frank, Miriam, Marilyn Ziebarth, and Connie Field. *The Life and Times of Rosie the Riveter: The Story of Three Million Working Women during World War II*. Emeryville, CA: Clarity Educational Productions, 1982.

Gilman, Charlotte Perkins. *The Yellow Wallpaper*. Ed. Dale M. Bauer. Boston and New York: Bedford Books, 1998.

Glancy, Mark. *When Hollywood Loved Britain: The Hollywood "British" Film 1939–1945*. Manchester; New York: Manchester University Press; Distributed exclusively in the USA by St. Martin's Press, 1999.

Glaspell, Susan. "A Jury of Her Peers," *A Pocketful of Prose: Vintage Short Fiction, Volume II.* Ed. David Madden. Fort Worth, TX: Harcourt Brace & Company, 1996. 176–92.

Gledhill, Christine, *"Klute* 2: Feminism and *Klute,"* *Women in Film Noir.* Ed. E. Ann Kaplan. London: British Film Institute, 1978. 112–28.

Gluck, Shema Berger. *Rosie the Riveter Revisited: Women, the War, and Social Change.* Boston: Twayne, 1987.

Golden, Eve. *Vamp: The Rise and Fall of Theda Bara.* Vestal, NY: Emprise Pub., 1996.

Gorman, Edward, Lee Server, and Martin Harry Greenberg (eds). *The Big Book of Noir.* New York: Carrol and Graf, 1998.

Grossman, Julie. "The Trouble with Carol: The Costs of Feeling Good in Todd Haynes' s *[Safe]* and the American Cultural Landscape," *Other Voices: The (e)Journal of Cultural Criticism* 2.3 (2005).

Gunning, Tom. *The Films of Fritz Lang: Allegories of Vision and Modernity.* London: British Film Institute, 2000.

Haggard, H. Rider. *Three Adventure Novels.* New York: Dover Publications, 1951.

Hanson, Helen. *Hollywood Heroines: Women in Film Noir and the Female Gothic Film.* London: I. B. Tauris, 2007.

Hardy, Thomas. *Tess of the D'Urbervilles.* London; New York: Penguin Books, 1978.

——. *The Well-Beloved.* Oxford; New York: Oxford University Press, 1986.

——. *Far from the Madding Crowd.* New Wessex ed. New York: St. Martin's Press, 1977.

——. *Jude the Obscure.* 2001 Modern Library pbk. ed. New York: Modern Library, 2001.

Harman, Barbara Leah and Susan Meyer. *The New Nineteenth Century: Feminist Readings of Underread Victorian Fiction.* New York: Garland Pub., 1996.

Harvey, Sylvia. "Woman's Place: The Absent Family of Film Noir." *Women in Film Noir.* Ed. E. Ann Kaplan. London: British Film Institute, 1978. 22–34.

Haskell, Molly. *From Reverence to Rape: The Treatment of Women in the Movies.* 2nd ed. Chicago: University of Chicago Press, 1987.

Heller, Tamar. "The Vampire in the House: Hysteria, Female Sexuality, and Female Knowledge in Le Fanu's 'Carmilla' (1872)," *The New Nineteenth Century: Feminist Readings of Underread Victorian Fiction.* Ed. Barbara Leah Harman and Susan Meyer. New York and London: Garland Publishing, 1996. 77–95.

Hirsch, Joshua. "Film Gris Reconsidered," *Journal of Popular Culture* 34.2 (2006). 82–93.

Hirsch, Foster. *The Dark Side of the Screen: Film Noir.* 1st ed. San Diego; London: A. S. Barnes; Tantivy Press, 1981.

——. *Detours and Lost Highways: A Map of Neo-Noir.* 1st Limelight ed. New York: Limelight Editions, 1999.

Hollinger, Karen. *"Film Noir,* Voice-Over, and the Femme Fatale," *Film Noir Reader.* Ed. Alain Silver and James Ursini. New York: Limelight, 1996. 242–59.

Hoyt, Clark. "Pantsuits and the Presidency," *New York Times,* June 22, 2008.

Hudson, Jennifer. "'No Hay Banda, and Yet We Hear a Band': David Lynch's Reversal of Coherence in *Mulholland Drive,"* *Journal of Film and Video* 56.1 (2004). 17–24.

Isenberg, Noah William. *Detour.* Houndmills, Basingstoke, Hampshire; New York: Palgrave Macmillan, 2008.

James, Henry. *The Turn of the Screw*. New York and London: W. W. Norton and Company, 1966.

——. *The Portrait of a Lady*. New York: Modern Library, 1951.

Jameson, Fredric. *Postmodernism, Or, the Cultural Logic of Late Capitalism*. Durham: Duke University Press, 1991.

Johnston, Claire. "Myths of Women in the Cinema," *Women and the Cinema: A Critical Anthology*. Ed. Karyn Kay and Gerald Peary. New York: E. P. Dutton, 1977. 407–11.

Kael, Pauline. "Circles and Squares," *Film Quarterly* 16: 3 (Spring, 1963). 12–26.

Kaplan, E. Ann. "Is the Gaze Male," *Women and Film: Both Sides of the Camera*. New York: Methuen, 1983. 23–35.

——. "The Place of Women in Fritz Lang's *The Blue Gardenia*," *Women in Film Noir*. Ed. E. Ann Kaplan. London: British Film Institute, 1998. 81–8.

——. *Women and Film: Both Sides of the Camera*. New York: Methuen, 1983.

——. *Women in Film Noir*. London: British Film Institute, 1978; Rev. ed. 1998.

Kast, Pierre. "A Brief Essay on Optimism," *Perspectives on Film Noir*. Ed. R. Barton Palmer. New York: G. K. Hall and Company, 1953; 1996. 44–9.

Kay, Karyn and Gerald Peary (eds). *Women and the Cinema: A Critical Anthology*. E. P. Dutton, 1977.

Kemp, Philip. "From the Nightmare Factory: HUAC and the Politics of Noir," *The Big Book of Noir*. Ed. Edward Gorman, Lee Server, and Martin Harry Greenberg. New York: Carrol and Graf, 1998.

Kitses, Jim. *Gun Crazy*. London: British Film Institute, 1996.

Knobloch, Susan. "Sharon Stone's (An)Aesthetic," *Reel Knockouts: Violent Women in the Movies*. Ed. Martha McCaughey and Neal King. Austin: University of Texas Press, 2001. 124–44.

Krutnik, Frank. *In a Lonely Street: Film Noir, Genre, Masculinity*. London; New York: Routledge, 1991.

Kucich, John and Diane Sadoff (eds). *Victorian Afterlife*. Minneapolis/London: University of Minnesota Press, 2000.

Landy, Marcia (ed.). *Imitation of Life: A Reader on Film and Television Melodrama*. Wayne State University Press, 1991.

Leave Her To Heaven. Press Book, British Film Institute National Library, 1945.

Ledger, Sally and Roger Luckhurst (eds). *The Fin De Siecle: A Reader in Cultural History c. 1880–1900*. Oxford and New York: Oxford University Press, 2000.

Lentzner, Jay R. and Donald R. Ross. "The Dreams that Blister Sleep: Latent Content and Cinematic Form in *Mulholland Drive*," *American Imago* 62.1 (2005). 101–23.

Levine, Philippa. *Feminist Lives in Victorian England: Private Roles and Public Commitment*. Oxford: Basil Blackwell, 1990.

Liebman, Nina C. "Piercing the Truth: Mildred and Patriarchy," *Literature in Performance* 8.1 (1988). 39–52.

Linehan, Marsha M. *Cognitive-Behavioral Treatment of Borderline Personality Disorder*. 2005 ed. London: Faber and Faber, 1997.

Littau, Karin. "Refractions of the Feminine: The Monstrous Transformations of Lulu," *MLN*, Volume 110, Number 4, September 1995 (Comparative Literature Issue), pp. 888–912.

MacCannell, Dean. "Marilyn Monroe Was Not a Man," *Diacritics* 17.2 (1987). 114–27.

Madden, David (ed.). *A Pocketful of Prose: Vintage Short Fiction, Volume II*. Fort Worth, TX: Harcourt Brace & Company, 1996.

Maguire, Gregory. *Wicked: The Life and Times of the Wicked Witch of the West*. New York: HarperCollins, 1995.

Marcus, Jane. "Salome: The Jewish Princess Was a New Woman," *Bulletin of the New York Public Library* 78 (1974). 95–113.

Martin, Angela. "'Gilda Didn't Do Any of Those Things You've been Losing Sleep Over!': The Central Women of 40s Film Noir," in Kaplan (ed.) *Women in Film Noir* (1998). 202–28.

Martin, Adrian. "Violently Happy: Gun Crazy (1950)," in *Film Noir Reader 4*. 83–6.

Maxfield, James F. *The Fatal Woman: Sources of Male Anxiety in American Film Noir, 1941–1991*. Madison; London: Fairleigh Dickinson University Press; Associated University Presses, 1996.

McArthur, Colin. *The Big Heat*. London: British Film Institute, 1992.

McGowan, Todd. "Lost on *Mulholland Drive*: Navigating David Lynch's Panegyric to Hollywood," *Cinema Journal* 43.2 (2004). 67–89.

McNamara, Eugene. "Preminger's *Laura* and the Fatal Woman Tradition," *Clues* 3.2 (1982). 24–9.

Mildred Pierce. Press Book, British Film Institute National Library, 1945.

Modleski, Tanya. *Feminism Without Women: Culture and Criticism in a Postfeminist Age*. New York: Routledge, 1991.

Morrison, Susan (ed.). *Thirty Ways of Looking at Hillary*. New York: HarperCollins Publishers, 2008.

Muller, Eddie. *Dark City: The Lost World of Film Noir*. 1st St. Martin's ed. New York: St. Martin's Griffin, 1998.

Mulvey, Laura. *Citizen Kane*. London: British Film Institute, 1992.

——. *Visual and Other Pleasures*. Bloomington, Indiana: Indiana University Press, 1989.

——. "Visual Pleasure and Narrative Cinema," *Screen* 16.3 (1975). 6–18, reprinted in *Visual and Other Pleasures*.

Naremore, James. *More than Night: Film Noir in its Contexts*. Berkeley: University of California Press, 1998.

Neale, Steve. *Genre and Hollywood*. London; New York: Routledge, 2000.

Nelson, Carolyn Christensen (ed.). *A New Woman Reader*. Toronto: Broadview Press, 2001.

Nochimson, Martha P. "*Mulholland Drive*," *Film Quarterly* 56.1 (2002). 37–45.

——. "'All I Need is the Girl': The Life and Death of Creativity in *Mulholland Drive*," *The Cinema of David Lynch: American Dreams, Nightmare Visions*. Ed. Erica Sheen and Annette Davison. New York and London: Wallflower Press, 2005. 165–81.

Noonan, Peggy. "Can Mrs. Clinton Lose," *The Wall Street Journal*, February 8, 2008: W14.

Novak, Phillip. "The *Chinatown* Syndrome," *Criticism* 49.3 (2007). 255–83.

Oliver, Kelly and Benigno Trigo. *Noir Anxiety*. Minneapolis: University of Minnesota Press, 2003.

Palmer, R. Barton. *Perspectives on Film Noir*. New York; London: G. K. Hall; Prentice Hall International, 1996.

Petro, Patrice. *Joyless Streets: Women and Melodramatic Representation in Weimar Germany*. Princeton, NJ: Princeton University Press, 1989.

Pitfall. Press Book, British Film Institute National Library, 1948.

Place, Janey. "Women in Film Noir," *Women in Film Noir*. Ed. E. Ann Kaplan. London: British Film Institute, 1998. 47–68

Polan, Dana B. *In a Lonely Place*. London: British Film Institute, 1993.

Porfirio, Robert, Alain Silver, and James Ursini. *Film Noir Reader 3: Interviews with Filmmakers of the Classic Noir Period*. 1st Limelight ed. New York: Limelight Editions, 2002.

Rafter, Nicole Hahn. *Shots in the Mirror: Crime Films and Society*. Oxford; New York: Oxford University Press, 2000.

Rich, B. Ruby. "Dumb Lugs and Femme Fatales," *Sight and Sound* 5.11 (1995). 6–10.

——. "Twin Peaks (Review of *Mulholland Drive*)," *The Nation*. November 12, 2001.

Richardson, Angelique and Chris Willis, *The New Woman in Fiction and in Fact*. New York: Palgrave Macmillan, 2002.

Ricks, Christopher B. *The New Oxford Book of Victorian Verse*. Oxford; New York: Oxford University Press, 1987.

Riquelme, John Paul. "Shalom/Solomon/Salome. Modernism and Wilde's Aesthetic Politics," *The Centennial Review* 39 (1995). 575–619.

Rodley, Chris (ed.). *Lynch on Lynch* (revised edition). London: Faber and Faber, 2005.

Schatz, Thomas. *Boom and Bust: American Cinema in the 1940s*. Berkeley and Los Angeles: University of California Press, 1997.

Schrader, Paul. "Notes on *Film Noir*" (1972). *Film Noir Reader*. Ed Alain Silver and James Ursini. 7th Limelight ed. New York: Limelight Editions, 1996. 52–63.

Seelye, Katharine Q. and Julie Bosman, "Media Charged with Sexism in Clinton Coverage," *New York Times*, June 13, 2008.

Senf, Carol A. *The Vampire in Nineteenth-Century English Literature*. Bowling Green State University Popular Press, 1988.

Server, Lee, Edward Gorman, and Martin Harry Greenberg. *The Big Book of Noir*. 1st Carroll & Graf ed. New York: Carroll & Graf Publishers, 1998.

Sheen, Erica and Annette Davison (eds). *The Cinema of David Lynch: American Dreams, Nightmare Visions*. New York and London: Wallflower Press, 2005.

Shetley, Vernon. "The Presence of the Past: *Mulholland Drive* Against *Vertigo*," *Raritan* 25.3 (2006). 112–28.

Showalter, Elaine. *Sexual Anarchy: Gender and Culture at the Fin De Siecle*. New York: Penguin, 1990.

Silver, Alain and James Ursini. *Film Noir Reader*. 7th Limelight ed. New York: Limelight Editions, 1996.

——. *Film Noir Reader 4*. 1st limelight ed. Pompton Plains NJ; Milwaukee, WI: Limelight Editions; Distributed by Hal Leonard, 2004.

——. *The Noir Style* (Woodstock, New York: The Overlook Press, 1999).

Silver, Alain and Elizabeth Ward. *Film Noir: An Encyclopedic Reference to the American Style*. Rev. and expand ed. Woodstock, NY: Overlook Press, 1988.

Smith, Grahame. *Dickens and the Dream of Cinema*. Manchester: Manchester University Press, 2003.

Smith, Murray. "*Film Noir* and the Female Gothic and *Deception*," *Wide Angle* (Vol 10, no. 1 (1988). 62–75.

Snyder, Scott. "Personality Disorder and the Film Noir Femme Fatale," *Journal of Criminal Justice and Popular Culture* 8.3 (2001). 155–68.

Sova, Dawn B. *Women in Hollywood: From Vamp to Studio Head*. 1st Fromm International ed. New York: Fromm International, 1998.

Spicer, Andrew. *European Film Noir*. Manchester, UK; New York: Manchester University Press; Distributed exclusively in the USA by Palgrave, 2007.

Spoto, Donald. *The Art of Alfred Hitchcock: Fifty Years of His Motion Pictures*. Garden City, NY: Doubleday, 1976.

Stacey, Jackie. *Star-Gazing: Hollywood Cinema and Female Spectatorship*. London; New York: Routledge, 1994.

Staiger, Janet. *Bad Women: Regulating Sexuality in Early American Cinema*. Minneapolis: University of Minnesota Press, 1995.

Stam, Robert. *Reflexivity in Film and Literature: From Don Quixote to Jean-Luc Godard*. New York: Columbia University Press, 1992.

Stoker, Bram and Leonard Wolf. *Dracula*. New York: Signet Classic, 1992.

Stott, Rebecca. *The Fabrication of the Late-Victorian Femme Fatale: The Kiss of Death*. Basingstoke: Palgrave Macmillan, 1992.

Thomas, Ronald R. "Specters of the Novel: *Dracula* and the Cinematic Afterlife of the Victorian Novel," *Victorian Afterlife*. Ed. John Kucich and Diane Sadoff. Minneapolis/London: University of Minnesota Press, 2000.

Tilove, Jonathan. "Hillary Hatred Finds its Misogynistic Voice," 2007. January 28, 2008. <http://www.newhouse.com/hillary-hatred-finds-its-misogynistic-voice.html>.

Toles, George. "Auditioning Betty in *Mulholland Drive*," *Film Quarterly*, September 2004, vol. 54, no. 1. 2–13.

Tomasky, Michael. "No Shame, No Gain," guardian.co.uk, June 4, 2008, accessed on January 5, 2009.

Turin, Maureen, "Flashbacks and the Psyche in Melodrama and Film Noir," in *Flashbacks in Film*. New York: Routledge, 1989.

Vicinus, Martha. *Independent Women: Work and Community for Single Women, 1850–1920*. Chicago and London: University of Chicago Press, 1985.

Wager, Jans B. *Dames in the Driver's Seat: Rereading Film Noir*. 1st ed. Austin: University of Texas Press, 2005.

——. *Dangerous Dames: Women and Representation in the Weimar Street Film and Film Noir*. Athens: Ohio University Press, 1999.

Waldman, Diane. "There's More to a Positive Image than Meets the Eye," *Issues in Feminist Film Criticism*. Ed. Patricia Erens. Indiana University Press, 1990. 13–18.

Walkowitz, Judith R. *City of Dreadful Delight: Narratives of Sexual Danger in Late-Victorian London*. Chicago: University of Chicago Press, 1992.

Walker, Michael, "Robert Siokmak," *The Book of Film Noir*, ed. Ian Cameron. New York: Continuum, 1993. 110–51.

"Whirlpool" (review). *Monthly Film Bulletin*, Vol. 18, 1951. 282.

Woolf, Virginia. "Professions for Women," *The Norton Anthology of English Literature*. Ed. M. H. Abrams, Jack Stillinger, and George Ford. 6th ed. New York and London: W.W. Norton, 1993. 1986–90.

Woolf, Virginia. *Mrs. Dalloway*. San Diego; New York; London: Harcourt Brace Jovanovich, 1925, 1981.

——. *A Room of One's Own*. New York: Harcourt Brace Jovanovich, 1981.

Žižek, Slavoj. "From 'Passionate Attachments' to Dis-Identification." <http://www.gsa.buffalo.edu/lacan/zizekidentity.htm>.

Index